David R. Bird was born during WWII in West London. At the age of 18, tired of Britain's climate and a job that was going nowhere, he impulsively joined the British South Africa Police in Southern Rhodesia and this was the beginning of a life of travel that resulted in his living in five different countries, visiting over forty, and traveling the world. He has been both a civil servant and an entrepreneur, experienced many highs and lows, and believes that each encounter has played a part in creating the ordinary man he is today.

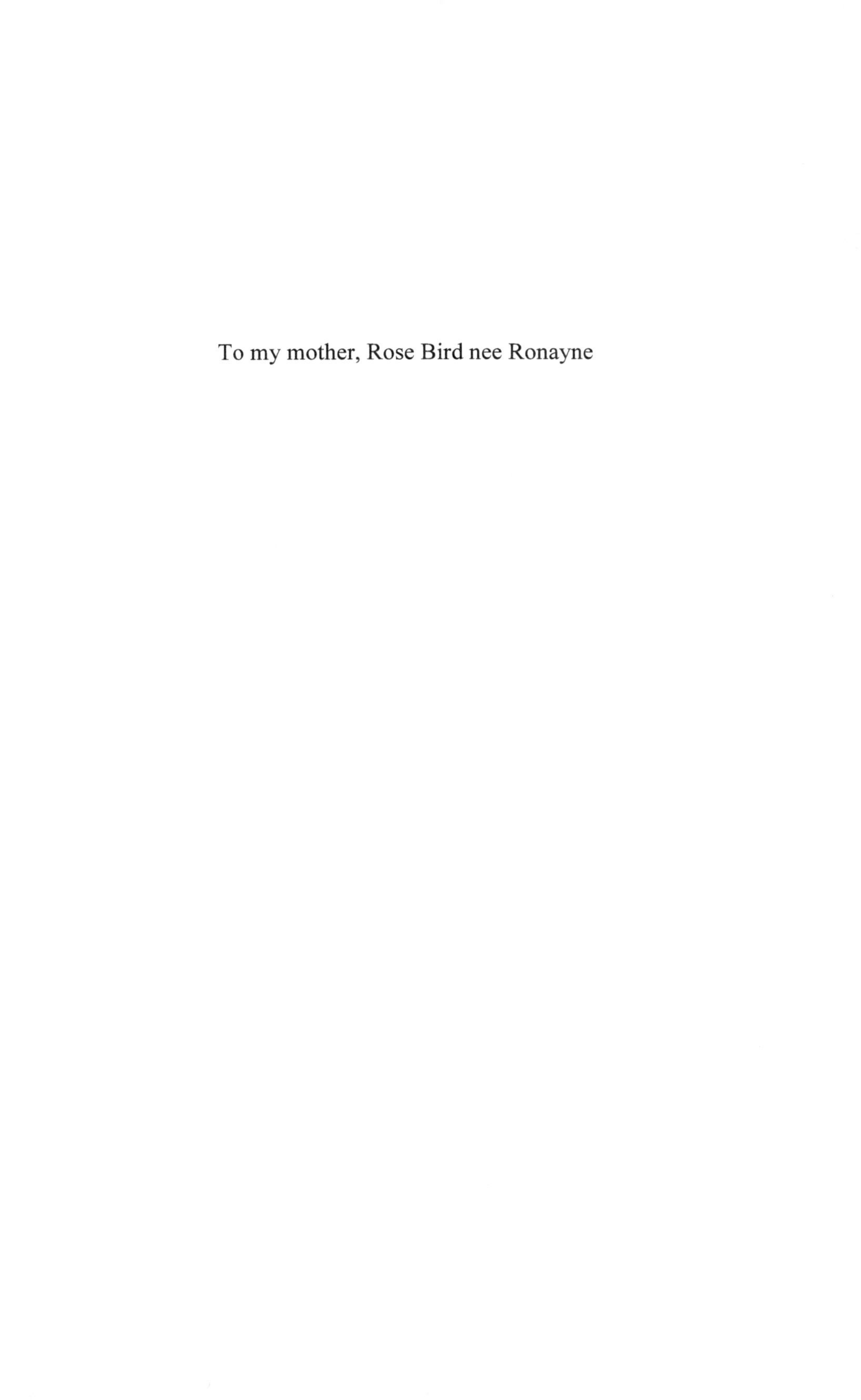

To my mother, Rose Bird nee Ronayne

David R. Bird

AN ORDINARY MAN

AUSTIN MACAULEY PUBLISHERS™

LONDON * CAMBRIDGE * NEW YORK * SHARJAH

Ordering Information
Quantity sales: Special discounts are available on quantity purchases by corporations, associations, and others. For details, contact the publisher at the address below.

Publisher's Cataloging-in-Publication data
Bird, David R.
An Ordinary Man

ISBN 9798891550674 (Paperback)
ISBN 9798891550681 (Hardback)
ISBN 9798891550698 (ePub e-book)

Library of Congress Control Number: 2023921368

www.austinmacauley.com/us

First Published 2024
Austin Macauley Publishers LLC
40 Wall Street, 33rd Floor, Suite 3302
New York, NY 10005
USA

mail-usa@austinmacauley.com
+1 (646) 5125767

I must thank my wife, Bonnie, for all her help, support, and encouragement and my editor, Carol Anderson-McLean, for all her advice and patience in helping this book to reach publication.

Foreword

This book was not written as a guide to how ordinary men should live their lives, God forbid. It's simply an attempt to tell the story of one ordinary man doing a collection of ordinary things that, when lumped together, might seem quite interesting to some.

Everyone has a story to tell. We all entered this world totally clueless, had our successes and failures, adventures and disappointments and along the way developed personal points of view that either coincided or clashed with those of others.

David tried to recall, as accurately as he could, the many anecdotes he encountered during his journey. None were exaggerated and many more were either forgotten or deliberately omitted.

He constantly reminds himself that many people have achieved far more than he has ever dreamed of. Athletes, statesmen, artists and everyday people from all walks of life have experienced and achieved far more—hence the title, *An Ordinary Man*.

He has enjoyed writing this book and has chosen to do so in the third person in order to avoid using the word 'I' in virtually every sentence. It could easily have been written as Book One—the events leading up to 1993, and Book Two—all that followed because he truly believes that 1993 began a new chapter in his life.

It must be stressed that although the colonialism of the 1960s and 1970s in no way resembles current ideology, this account is factual, truthful and accurate in the way he found things during that period. In another 50 or 60 years, people will probably take a dim view of life in today's world. Some already do.

This book may be of interest to future generations who may be fascinated to read of life as it really was in London and in colonial Africa in the 1950s and 1960s, just as he was when reading about the days of discovery and adventure during the eighteenth and nineteenth centuries.

What he does hope is that the future world continues its quest to venture farther into the unknown and continue to explore the infinity of space and the depths of the deepest oceans. Those things offer a wealth of opportunity if ordinary men and women have the guts and determination to take the initiative.

Two things are certain. The first is that during one lifetime everyone faces many forks in the road and whichever path is taken will result in a totally different outcome. The second harkens back to the old saying, 'Fools rush in where angels fear to tread', and on that score, he's presumably a fool!

Chapter One

On the first day of August, 1944, with World War II winding down and Germany's hopes of world domination looking pretty dim, London's Queen Charlotte Maternity Hospital was churning out newly born Londoners on a conveyer belt. One lucky seven-pounder, later to be christened David Richard Bird, was one of them.

The second son of George and Rose (Rosina) Bird, David went home in a London taxicab to their rented terrace house on Bloemfontein Road, Shepherd's Bush, London, W12.

Rose's parents, James and Mary Ronayne, occupied most of the upstairs although David and his older brother, John, occupied the upstairs front bedroom. Mom and Dad's bedroom was on the ground floor along with the kitchen, scullery, hallway, outdoor lavatory and a nicely furnished front room, which was hardly used except for entertaining important guests and the infrequent party.

The walled back garden had a rockery, a large and prolific pear tree, an equally prolific blackberry bush, a shed that, at some stage, had become home to half a dozen caged chickens and an air-raid shelter.

When the house was built, in the very early 20th century, the architect must have had in mind an occupant far more affluent than the Birds for in every room, next to the fireplace, a porcelain handle linked to a cable had been installed, which in turn was connected to a box in the kitchen. When the handle was turned, a bell rang in the kitchen and a red disc appeared in a little window in the box showing the servant to which room he or she was being summoned.

Shepherd's Bush was far west of London at that time, and there are two schools of thought as to how it got its name. The first was that when sheep farmers drove their sheep into London to feed the multitude, they had to make several overnight stops along the way. At that time, the area, now known as

Shepherd's Bush, was just an open area of countryside with plenty of wide-open grazing land for the shepherds and the sheep to rest, hence the name.

The second school of thought was that the same area of land was on the transit route for many carriages carrying wealthy passengers to and from London and was a favorite haunt for the renowned highwayman, robber and thief Jack Sheppard.

The highwayman would conceal himself behind some convenient shrubbery until a likely candidate appeared, whereupon he would reveal himself, brandish his pistols and relieve the passengers of their valuables. He was eventually caught and hanged at Tyburn.

It's David's belief that, in fact, both were the case. The arch-criminal Jack Sheppard did, in fact, exist and Londoners did, and still do, eat lamb…and the sheep had to get there somehow!

More recently, as London spread in all directions, what was once farmland or forest was developed and when Shepherd's Bush and, in particular, the Bloemfontein Road area was developed, the Anglo-Boer War (more commonly known as the Boer War) had just ended. This war was pitted between the Dutch settlers or Afrikaners, who were basically farmers, against the British Empire, which was more interested in commerce and industry.

This hard-fought war lasted from 1899 until 1902, and although the British eventually won, the Boers gave better than they got and to this day still hold a bitter grudge against their former foe.

With the Boer War still fresh in the minds of the British people, many of the roads such as Bloemfontein Road in the new development were named after towns and battles in South Africa.

As David grew, Britain was slowly recovering from the misery and destruction wrought by Adolph Hitler and his Nazi war machine. Their air-raid shelter on Bloemfontein Road was removed, food rationing was slowly eliminated and bomb-damaged Shepherd's Bush began clearing the debris and rebuilding.

The house directly across the street from their house was entirely demolished by a Nazi bomb during an air-raid in 1942 or thereabouts. All their front windows were blown in, but Brother John, who was about seven at the time, was asleep in his upstairs front bedroom and didn't even wake up.

The occupants of the destroyed house were killed when the bomb struck, but their parrot survived and Mom and Dad looked after it until they found it a new home.

As a young boy, David heard time and time again of the bombing and how one of his uncles, living a few streets away, hearing the blast and fearing the worst, came rushing over during the air-raid, relieved to discover that all was well at the Bird's household. What a close call!

One of David's earliest memories was of the weekly visit of one of his aunts who arrived after lunch, commonly called dinner in the U.K., as it was the main meal of the day, for a cup of tea with Mom every Friday afternoon and always bringing some biscuits, which often included ginger nuts or chocolate-covered digestives.

David would curl up on the rug in front of the coal-fired kitchen range, pretending to be asleep but in reality, he was listening to every word of gossip that the two women shared.

The visiting aunt was Irish and a staunch Roman Catholic, never missing an opportunity to attend Mass. The Bird family, who were all Church of England, rarely attended church. She was, however, a jovial soul and quite talkative about her fellow worshippers and her Reverend Father.

David's first day of school was something of a disaster. Ellerslie Road Infant and Primary School was just around the corner from Bloemfontein Road, and in the late summer of 1949, David was dutifully escorted there by his mother for his first day of formal education. He didn't want to go and screamed and cried the whole morning. He escaped during lunch hour, walking home much to the consternation of Mom, who once again marched him back to school.

The year 1949 proved to be a disaster for David, as shortly after the school incident—in September to be exact—Mom and Dad came home in a London taxicab with a baby, his newly arrived and soon-to-be-named sister, Linda.

Not really understanding how this had come about, he watched warily as this interloper to the family gained attention. Neighbors would come calling, billing and cooing, and generally making a big fuss of the new addition to the family. Aunts and uncles, Granny and Granddad, all did their bit to welcome Linda into the world and the only explanation that David ever received was that she was found under a gooseberry bush.

After spending the first few months of her life in a cot in Mom and Dad's bedroom, she was eventually moved into the front room. Upon reflection, David thought this was not a bad idea, as the room was hardly ever used except on the odd occasion when he would like to have used it to play with his electric train set or have a rough and tumble with his pals on a cold winter's day. The front room was now off limits at night-time or when Linda was put to bed for a nap.

Finally, David came to the understanding that school was to be his future for what seemed to be an eternity, and he began making friends. A young boy named Eddie, whose house backed on to his, was a classmate and became his best friend. They could climb the brick wall that separated the two gardens, and if they walked a short way along the wall, they came to another garden where some children of similar age lived.

They had a large shed with a flat corrugated iron roof that became a regular meeting place, although their father, a rather stern sergeant in the territorial army, didn't approve and regularly chased them off.

With Eddie came a bonus. He had no brothers or sisters, but something even better. He had a dog! Chuffy became one of the gangs and frequently joined them on the roof, much to the chagrin of the sergeant.

Other friends soon joined David's select group. All were boys and interested in a variety of intellectual pursuits, such as marbles (played in street gutters), conkers (horse chestnuts) on a string which were smashed against the opponent's conker with the aim of pulverizing it and five-stones (small square stones tossed in the air and caught on the back of the same hand).

A favorite pastime was going to the toilet, which was in the school playground and had no roof. Boys would line up against the trough-like urinal and see who could pee the highest. The real champs could sometimes pee right over the wall and howled with laughter when they heard the boys on the other side squeal in protest.

Girls were something of a mystery to David from the age of seven. Although his junior school was co-ed, the boys and girls had separate playgrounds. He and his friends considered girls a complete waste of time. They were no good at sports and spent most of their time playing with skipping ropes or bouncing tennis balls off a wall to the tune of some stupid rhyme or rhythm.

One exception to David's group of male friends was the girl next door. It was this young lady who enlightened David as to the 'gooseberry bush' story, mainly in the back seat of her father's ancient Vauxhall.

Another eventful year was 1952, the year of Queen Elizabeth II's coronation. David well remembers all the pomp and ceremony, Union Jacks flying everywhere, and the pride that everyone took in their new queen. All the mailboxes were changed to read EIIR rather than GR and virtually everyone bought or was given a coronation mug.

David was given a rather fancy propelling pencil at school to commemorate the event, and shortly after the coronation, all the children at David's school were marched up to the Western Avenue to see the queen as she drove by, each child waving their small Union Jack flag. Coronation year was also the year that New Zealand's Sir Edmond Hilary conquered Mount Everest.

Shortly after the coronation, David bought a puppy with some saved pocket money. Going up to Petticoat Lane—a market where anything from second-hand false teeth to used (stolen?) goods could be purchased—one Saturday morning, David and his dad purchased a Corgi cross-breed puppy for the princely sum of ten shillings. Proudly cuddling the six-week-old puppy in his jacket on the train ride home, David named her Peggy after the pretty lady who owned the sweet shop at the top of the road.

As soon as he got home, David put Peggy on the living room floor, where she promptly peed. Mom's only comment was that she looked like a rat, and as she left the room, she accidentally shut Peggy's long tail in the door. The dog howled, the tail bled and David cried.

Peggy (the dog, not the sweet shop lady) became a favorite with the neighbors and family, and especially with the landlord, Mr. Everard, who called round once a month to collect the rent.

David's mother's two sisters and their families also lived in Shepherd's Bush and were regular visitors to Bloemfontein Road every Saturday afternoon to visit Granny and Granddad. It was family rather than friends who made up the weekly get-togethers.

The Queens Park Rangers football ground was just around the corner, and the uncles and Dad usually went to the weekly football game. Mom's sisters, nephews and nieces, altogether nine in all, counting David, John and Linda, became close friends and saw each other regularly.

Sometimes David and a couple of friends would climb over or crawl under the back fence of the football stadium to watch the game, but never paid the entrance fee. In those days, only one side of the stadium had seating; everyone else stood on a series of concrete steps. For some reason, the seating area was called the stands and the standing areas were called terraces!

Life in Shepherd's Bush became quite mundane. Gray skies, rain, the occasional snowfall in winter and London's famous fog were just an accepted fact of life. David recalls one night when returning home from visiting a friend, the fog, regularly referred to as a pea-souper, was so thick that he walked right into a lamppost.

When David was about eight years of age, his brother John received his call-up papers. At that time, in the mid-1950s, conscription was still in place and every man had to sign up for two year's national service in the navy, army or air force.

John chose the army, probably because it offered the opportunity to learn a trade, and signed up to serve for three years, rather than the compulsory two, in the Royal Electrical and Mechanical Engineers (R.E.M.E.). After spending a few months training in Colchester, he was posted to Bielefeld in Germany as part of the British forces on the Rhine.

With frequent periods of leave, John would always bring home gifts for David and Linda from West Germany. For Linda, it was always dolls and David clearly remembers a battery-operated, remote-controlled Mercedes Benz with headlights that switched on and off and a remote-controlled tank with sparks that flew out of the two machine guns mounted on either side of the turret.

In those years, toys in Britain were very crude and simple; these German-made toys, by comparison, were luxurious beyond belief.

David was so proud of John in his uniform and would always be up at the Shepherd's Bush tube station to greet him when he arrived home on leave. Soldiers were always encouraged, perhaps they were instructed, to wear uniforms when out in public and they didn't seem to mind. Perhaps they enjoyed the attention they received, especially from the fairer sex.

Every year, a searchlight tattoo was held at the nearby White City Stadium. This involved thousands of servicemen from all branches of the military, including massed bands drawn from a variety of regiments. Kilted highlanders, horse mounted Household Cavalry and Coldstream Guards in their bearskin busbies, artillery and helicopters were all there, and a large number made their way to the White City Stadium straight down Bloemfontein Road and right past their house.

There was one occasion when David recalls that John did not enjoy wearing his uniform. This was when he was home on leave and took David to the tattoo. "Never again," he remarked once they were back home. Apparently, he had spent most of his time saluting the multitude of officers in attendance.

At about this time, Mom encouraged David to join the local library in East Acton. The library was just over a mile away and on David's first visit, he came across some books in the children's section written by a woman author named Richmal Crompton.

The books, in fact, were a series of 38 that chronicled the adventures of an unruly schoolboy named William Brown—generally known as Just William.

Taking one of these books home, he soon discovered that William was a boy after his own heart and the more he read, the more engrossed he became in William's exploits. He couldn't put the book down, and when finished, he was off to the library searching for another book in the Just William series.

When he had exhausted the library's collection of Just William, he resorted to other authors and this time selected Enid Blyton's Famous Five series, the Famous Five consisting of two boys, Julian and Dick, two girls named Anne and George, and their dog Timmy.

After this, David became something of a bookworm, and to this day he prefers reading a book to watching television or engaging in other forms of entertainment. He offers his sincere thanks to the two ladies, Richmal Crompton and Enid Blyton, for helping to spark his sense of adventure, imagination and creativity.

As his school years progressed, David proved to be an average student with weekends, summer holidays and after-school activities of far more importance than English, math, history, science and geography, although geography was by far his favorite subject.

In his final years at junior school, at the age of 10 or 11, one of the teachers, a Scottish woman, decided that at the school's annual entertainment, to which all the parents were invited, David's class would put on a display of Scottish dancing. After months of rehearsals, with the teacher bringing along a box filled with her husband's sword collection, David and his male classmates learned to perform the sword dance.

They also had to dance with girls in the class performing the Gay Gordon's or some similar dance routine while wearing costumes made up of kilts, lace cuffs, neck ties and bright, fancy berets. Although in total denial, David quite enjoyed dancing with his partner that evening, for he'd never held a girl that close before and she was quite pretty.

Music had always been one of David's interests. Both his brother John and one of his aunts were accomplished harmonica players and David took up this instrument like a duck to water. He later learned to play the recorder and, at one point, went to Royal Albert Hall for an unsuccessful audition to join the all-England youth orchestra.

At the age of 11, every child in Britain was required to write an examination called the eleven plus. This would determine whether the child qualified for the higher level of secondary school, termed a Grammar school, from where suitable college or university education could result, or was sent to a secondary modern school where the riff-raff could complete their education.

Once the results were in, David and his mom went for a meeting at the school, where it was explained that while David did qualify for Grammar school, he had barely scraped through. A third level of secondary school was, however, being introduced—a Central school—and it was suggested that this was the school David should attend. Thus, his next five years of education were set.

His secondary school was boys only, and the wearing of school uniforms was strictly enforced. Whereas Primary school required short trousers, secondary school required long, gray flannel trousers, a school blazer and tie and a leather school satchel. He felt pretty good about the uniform.

The blazer's embroidered school badge was elaborate and colorful, the school tie was color-coded to identify the house that he was in (there were four houses, each identified by the colors red, blue, green or yellow and each were named after famous British poets), and the long trousers were the first he had ever owned and made him feel very grown up.

For recreation, a very used fixed-wheel bicycle improved transportation. Pocket money supplemented by a milk round every Saturday morning with milkman Bob provided sufficient funds to support his teenage requirements.

David found Bob to be a fascinating companion. They toured the neighborhood in an electric-powered milk float. Yes, a battery-operated milk float that carried the driver and one passenger and perhaps as many as 50 crates of milk bottles, and this was in the mid-1950s. Why has it taken so long to develop an electric car? Could the petrol companies and motor car manufacturers have had their fingers in the pie?

Milkman Bob was constantly smoking a pipe, a filthy thing that he frequently shook out to remove the dottle, but which David became accustomed to and eventually rather enjoyed the aroma. Bob had several stops along the route where they were invited indoors for a hot cup of tea and some biscuits or cake.

David clearly remembers their frequent visits to Mrs. Budd, who was especially nice to them both and had a daughter the same age as David. She always seemed to make sure that David and her daughter shared the same couch. David was still at the stage where he considered girls useless, so Mrs. Budd's efforts to play matchmaker, if that was what she intended, were wasted.

For many years, David enjoyed celebrating November 5th which was, of course, Guy Fawkes Day! Guy Fawkes's claim to fame occurred when he attempted to blow up the Houses of Parliament in 1605. Ever since then, the people of Britain have celebrated this infamous individual.

Some see him as a hero, but most consider him an urban terrorist whose ultimate demise is generally considered well deserved. In 1606, Mr. Fawkes was convicted and sentenced to be hung, drawn and quartered. He escaped the drawn and quartered bit by leaping in the air at the moment the noose tightened and broke his neck. Smart fellow.

Several centuries later, when David was on the scene, children would make life-sized dummies of Guy Fawkes, usually attaching an old pair of Dad's trousers to one of his old shirts and stuffing it with straw or an old newspaper. Mounted on top was a similarly stuffed bag to represent a head, which was then adorned with an ugly mask and hat.

The Guy was always made well ahead of November 5th and paraded around the neighborhood in an old pram, pushchair or wheelbarrow by children holding tin cans and calling 'Penny for the Guy'. The money thus collected was used to buy fireworks, and on the evening of November 5th bonfires was lit. Poor old Guy was burned at the stake and fireworks were set off all over Britain.

David and a few friends would position their guy outside the Shepherd's Bush railway station on Saturdays before the 5th, especially if there was a football match on, yelling 'Penny for the Guy' at the top of their lungs and shaking their tins. Consequently, they always had plenty of money for fireworks.

A similar group of children in the north of England were not so lucky. When touring the neighborhood with their very realistic-looking Guy, one of the children wearing a mask and dressed up to look authentic, the children were confronted by the local, jovial butcher who, in fun, hacked the Guy's head off with his butcher's hatchet.

David's cousins and friends were all involved in this annual event, and Mom and Dad always had a bonfire in the back garden, accompanied by fireworks and rockets. Aunts and uncles all came around, fireworks were going off all over London and thick smoke permeated the air from thousands of bonfires.

Chapter Two

Shortly after David started his secondary school education in Hammersmith, the Sir Christopher Wren Boys' School was built and opened in 1956. It was a convenient few minutes' walk, as it was also on Bloemfontein Road. This was to be David's final school and will always be remembered as a bright and modern campus with three fine gymnasiums and a magnificent auditorium that seated the entire school.

Rather than having one or two teachers who taught everything, secondary school was much more organized. Different classrooms and different teachers for different subjects. Discipline during all of David's school years was far stricter than it is today, both in primary, elementary and secondary schools.

Corporal punishment in the form of canings and after-school detention was liberally dished out and, in David's current opinion, was just and fairly administered, although he probably didn't approve of it at the time. Secondary school was, however, far stricter than he was used to and bred in its students a standard of behavior that would not go amiss in today's world.

***

Meanwhile, political unrest was building in Britain, particularly in London, and in August 1958, racial tension flared in West London. Most impoverished families were becoming alarmed at the large influx of Black immigrants occupying their neighborhoods, and complaints of 'they're coming over here and taking our jobs' were frequently heard.

Eventually, tempers rose to boiling point and in the nearby borough of Notting Hill, groups of Teddy Boys and unemployed thugs began attacking anyone considered a 'darkie', a term used in those days to refer to anyone with a black face.

The end result, after six days of intense rioting, was the arrest of more than 100 people, and the Notting Hill riots became a sad part of West London's history.

***

David had joined the Boy Scouts at the age of 11 and had made several new friends, including one very good school friend who, although not a scout, had a father who drove one of the familiar bright red double-decker London Transport buses and even more impressively had driven a tank during the war.

Scouting became David's first love for several years. Frequent camping expeditions gave him a taste for the outdoors and the countryside and instilled in him a spirit of adventure.

'The skipper', as his scoutmaster was referred to, was a tough war veteran still young enough to scale mountains and climb the highest trees. He and his wife had no children of their own, but he was hero-worshipped by the 12th Hammersmith scout troop and took them on many thrilling and exciting forays.

On one memorable scouting trip, they camped for a week in a farmer's field on the Isle of Sheppey, which lies on the southern side of the Thames estuary opposite Southend-On-Sea. His troop was loaded onto the open back of a five-ton lorry for the journey from London and back.

They cooked all their own meals, slept in tents and had a wonderful if somewhat dirty time climbing cliffs, building fires and learning the rudiments of being outdoorsmen.

Other scouting adventures included frequent weekends to places like Chalfont St. Peters, where the Boy Scouts owned a large tract of land with lakes, streams and woods. It was the perfect getaway for inner-city youngsters to get a taste of the great outdoors. There was no great expense involved in scouting.

Perhaps, a shilling a week at the scout meetings and the cost of the uniform. If the scout's family couldn't afford it, the weekly shilling attendance fee was waived and a uniform was provided.

Cycling became another of David's strong interests as he grew older. He would think nothing of a day's outing to Worthing, Southend or Brighton and back, a distance of 100 miles or so, with a group of like-minded friends.

Once, when he was 16, he cycled 800 miles along the coastal route from London to Land's End and back with his cousin Robert, their bikes loaded down with a tent, sleeping bags and cooking paraphernalia.

On this journey, they visited many of the small fishing villages that dotted the coastline, places with such crazy names as Beer Head, Bigbury Bay, Mevagissey and Mousehole before eventually reaching Land's End. One hiccup along the way was when David, while cycling through the New Forest during a heavy rainstorm, left the road and plowed straight into a deep storm drain, severely buckling his front wheel.

By a stroke of extraordinary good luck, a motorist in a van, who owned a bicycle shop in Christchurch, stopped when seeing the stranded cyclists, took them to his shop and straightened the wheel. They then continued on their merry way, finding a handy farmer's field and pitching their tent, usually eating a tin of corned beef for dinner and not feeling the least bit hard done by. At sunrise the following morning, they cooked eggs, bacon and ate corn flakes and were on their way exploring new and interesting places.

David's aunt Violet had told the two boys that in the unlikely event that they reached Land's End, they should call at the local post office, where there may be something waiting for them. The 'something' turned out to be 10 pounds, which saved their bacon, for they had almost run out of money.

Their route home was via the north coast of Devon and Cornwall, calling at King Arthur's Castle and the villages of Lynton and Lynmouth, which had recently suffered severe flooding. They also sampled some scrumpy (strong cider) with some of their 10 pounds while riding through the famous apple-growing county of Somerset, completing their 800-mile round trip in eight days.

Another one of his cycling companions was cousin Marion who, like him, owned a Carlton Catalina Special sports bike with anodized large flange hubs. Their cycling forays were of a more modest nature, perhaps Windsor or London Airport. These more sedate single-day outings, taking with them a sandwich and soft drink, were certainly more to her taste than the Land's End adventure.

***

Back at school, there was a decision to be made as to what career path to choose. Sir Christopher Wren School was termed a central school, somewhere between grammar and secondary modern, and specialized in preparing students to enter one of the trades.

The school gave each student a six-month taste of six different trades: carpentry, plumbing, metalwork, brickwork, technical drawing and interior decorating. David selected the latter and spent his final year of secondary school learning more about the interior decorator's trade.

In order to supplement the pocket money, he gratefully received from Dad every weekend, and with the milk round now beneath his dignity and not paying enough, David took a Saturday job at the Hammersmith Co-op, a large department store on King's Street in Hammersmith. He was in his final year at school, and approaching his school-leaving age of 16, David had his first girlfriend.

He'd had his eye on a very attractive girl working at the Co-op and eventually plucked up enough courage to ask her to go out with him. Being totally new to the dating game, he handled his proposal very badly. For one thing, the girl was about two years older than he was. However, she handled the situation very diplomatically, saying that although she was not available, she knew of another girl working at the cosmetics counter, whom she thought would be very interested.

The girl in question, who was still at school and only worked on Saturdays, attended the girls' school adjacent to his own, was his age and very pretty so after a brief introduction a date was set. Again, as David was new to the dating game, he felt that an appropriate date would be an evening at the cinema and a box of chocolates.

Following the film, David walked her home with the hope that he might be rewarded with a goodnight kiss. Beneath her porch light, she warned David to be very quiet as her father would not take kindly to any smooching. She then embraced him, smacked a soft and loving kiss right on his lips and stuck her tongue deep into his mouth.

David's legs went wobbly. Flabbergasted, his reaction was pathetic. He had never experienced or heard of such a thing, and in a slightly bemused state, he walked on air all the way home. Only later, when a classmate disclosed that he had previously dated the same girl, did he learn that many a suitor had tasted far greater delights than his one French kiss.

During the summer of 1960, David's brother, John, was married. His wife-to-be lived in Greenwich, which is in the East End of London, where their wedding was to be held. The bride's father had booked a large room over a local public house for the reception and David, thanks to Mom and Dad's generosity, had bought a new, hand-tailored suit for the occasion.

The bride and groom were driven from the church to the reception by John's best friend in his flashy black and white Sunbeam Talbot convertible. The reception was attended by close to 100 people, and the booze flowed freely. David sat with the bride's sister and her best friend and, during the course of the evening, became quite enamored with the best friend.

During the course of their conversation, David learned that she was the granddaughter of one of Britain's former prime ministers, namely David Lloyd George, who served from 1916 until 1922. He was a liberal politician from Wales who was famous for his support of a national homeland for the Jewish people in Palestine.

The East Enders, known to be a rough lot, lived up to their reputation when a fight broke out between the bride's father and one of her brothers. The brother was quickly ejected, but the bride was reduced to tears and David, who played no part in the disturbance or its resolution, attempted to impress the friend by declaring how he would have handled the situation if given the chance.

It should be noted that the offending brother, a tough military veteran of the Korean War, would have made mincemeat of David in about five seconds had he intervened.

However, David must have made some impression on the friend, for shortly afterwards, he received a postcard from her stating that she was staying at one of the Lloyd George properties in Wales if he would care to visit. He didn't respond and didn't visit, possibly blowing the opportunity of hobnobbing with the gentry!

***

Leaving school at 16 was quite normal. In fact, the school-leaving age was 15 and he had stayed on an extra year to acquire the necessary GCE's to gain admission to college. There was no such thing as graduation—that was only for university graduates. David and three friends, however, went out to celebrate by visiting the West End to see a show.

David had succeeded in gaining admission to the art department of the Brixton School of Building, with a view to becoming an interior designer and acquiring a National Diploma in Design (NDD) after four years of study.

There was no fee for attending the four-year full-time course and all began well, with the exception that while his friends had begun apprenticeships that paid a small salary, he had no income except for the small wage for working Saturdays at the Hammersmith Co-op.

Being a member of the student's union and being introduced to a different type or class of individual became something of an eye-opener. Many of his fellow students were from overseas, some from Nigeria on some sort of government-sponsored scheme, others from Persia with loads of money and who arrived at the college each morning in a shiny new Mercedes Benz.

There was even one girl from Siam (Thailand) who claimed to be a princess and was wrapped in robes of silk and satin. Another young man, considerably older than 16, came from Italy. The British contingent consisted of David, two other boys and three girls all about David's age.

The three English boys, each from working-class families, quickly became friends, but the girls were rather stuck up, being better educated and obviously more upper class.

It didn't take too long for one of David's instructors to comment on his artwork, saying, "If you want to paint something that looks like a photograph, save yourself the trouble. Just go out and buy a camera." From that point on, he attempted to paint with less detail and a little streak of impressionism.

David enjoyed the social activities associated with being a college student and became a fan of traditional jazz (trad) music, which was all the rage. Kenny Ball, Acker Bilk, the Dutch Swing College Band and the Dixieland jazz of that era is still his music of choice.

But, and here's the crunch, he was spending one and a half hours each way, each day, on the London underground system—rush hour both ways—crammed in with city workers, men in pinstripe trousers and bowler hats and attractive women in high heels and fashionable outfits. David still wore his old school blazer with the badge cut off and felt distinctly out of place.

After spending a few months in the initial stages of becoming an interior designer, David and his two friends became aware that most of the men on campus were rather effeminate and girly.

The three of them were not really familiar with homosexuality, and if the subject was ever raised, it was always referred to with derision. They couldn't figure out why men behaved in such a fashion and any enquiries made as to this strange behavior was met with comments such as 'stay away from that lot' and 'they're just queers'.

However, a few discrete enquiries revealed that interior design was like a magnet to this type of individual, and all three felt it was time for a rethink.

At the age of 17, he and his two English colleagues decided to leave college and seek alternative careers. David took up full-time employment with the Hammersmith Co-op, bought a motor scooter and at the invitation of another fellow employee, joined the Furnivall Sculling Club on the River Thames.

He also struck up a friendship with Tim, a young man who managed the Co-op's jewelry department. It was from Tim that he purchased his motor scooter and it was Tim who introduced him to his second girlfriend. Ronnie was a window dresser for a large boutique directly across the road from the Co-op; she was petite and pretty. Romance entered the picture and in David's eyes, this was a match made in heaven.

They dated for several weeks and David learned a little more about the opposite sex and began to realize that girls were not so stupid after all. Ronnie was fun to be around and, being a little older than David, took on the role of teacher. However, their affair was not to last, and once again, David, just like in the old sing-along song, felt like *The Little Black Bull Who Came Down from the Meadow*, and was cast adrift to seek new pastures.

***

David's first visit to the Furnivall Sculling Club was an experience he would prefer to forget. One of the members welcomed him to the club, showed him a single-scull, gave him a brief introduction as to how to scull and set him afloat. While David was attempting to balance the craft, which was about 26 feet long and one foot wide, the incoming tide swept him into a flock of swans who were clearly unimpressed.

As much as he tried, he couldn't maneuver his craft in the right direction, and as he drifted beneath Hammersmith Bridge, he was disturbed to see a bunch of Teddy Boys leaning over the side of the bridge, watching his predicament below.

Teddy Boys were a fad in London during the 50s and early 60s and were so named because of the Edwardian clothing they wore. Generally, they were thugs who took great pleasure in bullying lesser mortals and they were to be avoided when at all possible.

To add to his troubles, they began laughing and jeering, then began spitting on him with the end result being, of course, that he tipped over into the river Thames. He slowly dragged the scull back to the boathouse, feeling totally stupid and incompetent, where he was advised that he might be more suited to rowing in a more stable four- or eight-man shell.

Although Furnivall was primarily a sculling club, it also catered to sweep rowers. For those uninitiated with the sport of rowing, scullers use two blades or oars, one in each hand, whereas sweep rowers have a much longer blade and are part of a crew with each crew member using two hands on the one blade.

David enjoyed rowing rather than sculling after tipping into the dirty old Thames on more than one occasion. He thereafter spent every Sunday morning down on the river at Hammersmith rowing in an eight-man shell, followed by a pint or two of Watney's Red Barrel in the club bar.

His introduction to rowing was not in one of the long, sleek racing shells that one sees in the Oxford and Cambridge boat races each year or at the Olympic Games.

Instead, it was in a wide, short, clinker-built wooden boat with a coxswain/coach in the stern and four novice rowers in staggered seating, each with a 10-foot-long wooden oar and facing their coxswain/coach. This boat, an excellent craft for teaching the rudiments of rowing, was known as a tub four.

Over a series of outings, he was taught the rudiments, the terminology and the importance of the rowing sequence of legs, back, arms, away, arms, back, legs—repeat.

Once he'd got the hang of it, he was assigned to a crew that would row for several miles each way from Hammersmith Bridge east alongside the old tow path. It is interesting to note that the tow path, obviously no longer used by horses towing barges, became a favorite night-time walk for young lovers.

Quite frequently, a used French letter (condom) became entangled in a rower's blade, causing much hilarity and ribald comments and obviously destroying the crew's timing to the consternation of their coxswain.

As an aside, it should be noted that back in the fifties and early sixties, shops were closed on Sundays with the exception of the odd corner store, which was only allowed to sell milk, bread and newspapers. Shopping back in those days was mostly over-the-counter sales, as self-serve supermarkets were only just coming into vogue.

British currency consisted of pounds, shillings and pence, of which 20 shillings equaled one pound and 12 pence, or pennies, equaled one shilling.

Coins consisted of half-crowns (two shillings and sixpence), florins (two shillings), shillings, otherwise known as a bob, sixpences, otherwise known as a tanner, three pence, more commonly known as thruppenny bits, pennies, half pennies (ha' pennies) and farthings (one-quarter of a penny).

Very confusing for foreign visitors, but David's grandmother, who was quite comfortable with the old currency, refused to go shopping once decimalization reared its ugly head.

***

Having turned seventeen, he decided that his next career of choice was to join London's Metropolitan Police Force, but he discovered that the GCE 'O' levels that he had acquired to gain admittance to art college were of no use in becoming a police cadet. He therefore decided to sit for three more GCE 'O' level exams in English, mathematics and geography. With those qualifications, he would be accepted as a cadet at the age of 18; otherwise, he would have to wait until he was 19 to apply.

He attended night school for the three subjects, studied for several months, and failed all three. So much for early entry into the Metropolitan police!

***

On the social scene, soon after being dumped by Ronnie, and while on board a jazz boat with a few friends and about 100 revelers enjoying a cruise from Hammersmith to Battersea and back, he encountered a truly beautiful girl who was seated alone. He sat beside her and offered to buy her a drink. As they chatted, David learned that she was a model and with looks and a figure like that, it seemed quite plausible.

When they got up to dance, it became quite apparent why she had been sitting at the table all alone. She was about six foot three and dwarfed David, who at five foot ten felt like a midget beside her.

One of David's scouting friends, a good and lasting friend named Colin, had recently been on a scouting trip to Holland with his handicapped brother, and upon returning to England, he told David of the wonderful time he had and talked about a particularly wonderful girl he met. He said that she had a friend who would love an English pen pal and suggested that he and David go over there and hitchhike across Holland to the town of Zwolle, where the two girls lived.

David, always anxious for a new adventure, thought this was a grand idea and immediately applied for a passport. The two set forth on an overnight ferry from Harwich to the Hook of Holland, sharing a cabin with a very friendly British soldier on his way back from leave, who generously shared his supply of Newcastle Brown Ale with them. Once on Dutch soil, they began thumbing lifts.

This was easier said than done for Dutch motorists were obviously not too keen on giving lifts to scruffy foreigners with backpacks, even if they did have their Union Jacks on prominent display. Although they did succeed in cadging two lifts, they eventually decided that they were not going to reach Zwolle in a timely fashion and reluctantly took a train.

When they arrived in the pretty town of Zwolle, David found the girls just as delightful as promised. Both girls spoke very good English and they were accommodated at their parent's houses. A few days of sightseeing followed, all on bicycles, the boys doing all the hard work, while the girls sat on the back carriers.

The girl's parents were extremely kind and went out of their way to make their British guests welcome. Overall, David's impression of Holland was of a flat, well-groomed and cultivated country, ideal for cycling and populated with friendly and cheerful people.

David's pen pal-to-be and most of the Dutch people he encountered were very keen on traditional jazz, especially their own world-famous Dutch Swing College Band. Upon returning home, David began writing to his Dutch girlfriend and remained in contact for several months, but he never returned to Holland to see her again. His friend, on the other hand, ended up marrying his one and together they had three children.

While working at the Co-op, learning to row, and failing miserably at his studies, David also took up martial arts in the form of Judo and, to a lesser degree, Kendo, under the tuition of an elderly Japanese fifth Dan instructor,

Mr. Michiku. David learned to breakfall, to use an opponent's strength against them and to foil the aggressor with the minimum of effort.

This came in very handy when riding home on his motor scooter one rainy night. It had been a hard Judo session and he was bundled up against the cold and in somewhat of a hurry when, cornering too fast, the scooter slipped from under him and he found himself rolling down the road at about 40 miles per hour, doing breakfall after breakfall until he came to a stop, virtually uninjured save for a minor ankle injury, which the local hospital took care of the following day.

The scooter, a German-made 200cc TWN model, had careened off in a different direction, scattering a group of people waiting at a bus stop. Luckily none of them were injured and David was able to ride his battered but still ridable scooter home—very gingerly.

Another romantic encounter occurred when his friend Colin invited him to a dance in the city. He took David to this rather noisy affair, which was held in the canteen of one of the large tenant's office premises. Beer was flowing freely and there were plenty of women. A girl by the name of Sandra caught his eye and at the end of the evening, David walked her to the railway station where she caught the last train home to Sidcup, a town just south of London in Kent.

This relationship withstood the test of time and he frequently made the 90-minute journey to Sidcup on his motor scooter and even went so far as to bring Sandra to Shepherd's Bush to meet Mom and Dad. This was the one—no doubt about it! She lived with her attractive mother, whose husband was killed during the war.

David considered her to be old, but she was probably only in her late 30s or early 40s. He got on very well with the mother and, in retrospect, wondered if he should have dumped Sandra and gone out with her mother instead!

While working at the Co-op, selling TVs, radiograms and other electronic entertainment devices of that era, a temporary booth was set up next to his department promoting Goblin vacuum cleaners and tea makers, the latter a device to be placed on the bedside table. By preparing it ahead of time, an alarm clock would waken a person at the pre-determined time with a piping hot cup of tea. In 1962, this was a breakthrough in modern technology.

The Goblin booth was staffed by an attractive and well-presented middle-aged woman. She was slim, articulate, had a black belt in Judo and two cats, and had an immense effect on the remainder of David's life. Her name was Miss Dexter.

Chapter Three

David and Miss Dexter struck up an immediate friendship and he was fascinated by the woman's worldly ways, her personality and her experiences. She showed him photographs of herself in her younger days aboard a banana boat in the Caribbean and told him how she had traveled the world, describing the sights she'd seen and the people she had encountered.

They got on so well together that David should have enquired more into her past but was probably so caught up in talking about himself that the thought never crossed his mind. He didn't even learn her first name and she remain an enigma to this day.

Having just turned 18, he mentioned his plans to join London's Metropolitan Police Force when he turned 19 and she mentioned that she knew of a young man who had traveled to Southern Rhodesia to join the colonial police force there and she believed that the minimum age requirement was only 18. She said the young man had signed up for three years, met and married a farmer's daughter and returned to England at the end of his three-year term with his new bride.

He thought no more of it until one day she turned up with an application form to join the British South Africa Police (BSAP). David completed the form and mailed it off without giving it any more thought.

A couple of weeks later, a letter arrived at Bloemfontein Road, giving the date and time for an interview at Rhodesia House on the Strand. Not mentioning any of this to Mom or Dad, 18-year-old David turned up at the appointed time suitably attired in suit and tie and found two other young men in the waiting room.

One, a rather short and ruddy-faced but well-spoken individual with a posh accent; the other, the complete opposite—a large, down-to-earth type who said he was from Blackpool and whose current occupation was making Blackpool rock.

Rhodesia House was, of course, the Rhodesian embassy in London. A fairly ancient building with very high ceilings and containing a display of wonderful photographs of African game animals ranging from the large and beautiful Rhone antelope, the lion and the elephant to the smallest of antelope, such as the klipspringer and duiker.

Each of the interviewees, in turn, went into a large office with a Colonel Someone-or-Other. David told the colonel of his desire to become a member of the Metropolitan police but that the minimum age was 19. The colonel put that matter to rest, confirming that 18 was the requirement for the BSAP.

He went on to explain the duties and requirements of a police officer in Southern Rhodesia, stressing that much of the police work involved working with a population of almost 6 million Africans. Every recruit would first undergo six months of intense training in the police depot, where he would learn of the indigenous population's history, nature and foibles along with training in equitation, marksmanship, law, physical fitness and driving.

David left Rhodesia House clutching a very impressive booklet describing life in the BSAP. The photographs of mounted police officers clad in safari suits, of the modern city of Salisbury with several high-rise buildings and descriptions of horse patrols in the African bush took his breath away.

Considering that the furthest he had ever been away from London was to Land's End and four days in the Dutch town of Zwolle, he was feeling a little overawed and full of self-doubt. Was he really up to the challenge?

A few weeks later, David's mom came to the Co-op looking rather flustered.

"David, what have you been up to? A policeman has just been to the house looking for you. He wouldn't say what it was about, but you must go to see him at the local police station."

She handed him a piece of paper with the police constable's name on it.

He left straight away and saw the policeman in question, who told him that he was conducting a routine interview for Rhodesia House before he could be accepted into the British South Africa Police. He told him that everything was satisfactory and that the 'all clear' would be relayed to Rhodesia House. "Congratulations and welcome to the club," he said.

David can still clearly recall sitting at the kitchen table at teatime after Dad had returned home from work and breaking the news to the family.

"Where is Southern Rhodesia?" asked one.

"It's six thousand miles away. We'll never see you again," came from another and so on.

He realized that he hadn't really thought through the repercussions of Miss Dexter's helpfulness and had yet to break the news to the young lady in Sidcup.

A week later, he was subjected to a full medical examination by a Harley Street specialist and the following week a letter arrived containing a BOAC airline ticket to fly from London to Rhodesia's capital city, Salisbury, via Frankfurt and Nairobi on 7 November 1962 arriving at noon, 8 November. Attached was a list of the 14 fellow recruits who would be traveling with him.

He handed in his two-week notice at the Hammersmith Co-op and after a quick whip round by the staff, he was presented with a large hold all as a going away present.

A farewell party was hosted by Mom and Dad at their house on Bloemfontein Road. Friends and family gave David a grand send off to darkest Africa. Photographs and memories remind him of this day and the 20 interesting years he spent in Africa.

He paid a last visit to Sidcup and a tearful farewell followed. Promises were made, letters would be written, and eventually they would be together again, although how this was to be accomplished wasn't at all clear.

Mom, Dad and Linda accompanied David to London Airport's bus terminal in central London and over a cup of tea they bid each other a final farewell. Dad was never a demonstrative kind of man, but David clearly remembers the trace of a tear in his eye and a tremor in his lower lip as he shook David's hand firmly and bid him farewell, possibly for the last time.

Men didn't hug men in those days, at least not in Britain, and David has stuck with this all his life, believing that a handshake is quite sufficient. He recalls seeing another young man in the tearoom going through the same ordeal, although his young sister was hysterical with grief. Linda was quite stoic...and possibly delighted?

The flight on a Boeing 707 was David's first experience of flying and he was duly impressed. Everyone was well dressed, the men wearing jackets and ties and the ladies in pretty frocks. The air hostesses were young, attractive and very attentive and the food very good.

David was especially fussy about his hair, which was fashionably cut in the Tony Curtis/Elvis Presley style with a D.A. ('duck's arse'), which for the uninitiated is greasy hair with the sides swept back until meeting in a similar style to the plumage of a duck's rear end.

David met up with a few fellow recruits at the stopovers in Frankfurt and Nairobi. He hooked up with the young man whose sister had been so overwrought at the airport terminal, and in the bar at Nairobi airport, he was introduced to a new beverage—vodka and lime juice! During his short stopover in Nairobi, David was fascinated by the view from the airport lounge.

Brilliant sunshine and bright blue skies overhead were something he was unaccustomed to and African personnel at the airport were so attentive, quite unlike the surly people he encountered seeing at London Airport. He even relaxed in a comfortable chair to have his shoes shined for a mere pittance.

Their flight arrived on time at Salisbury's small airport and having collected his Hammersmith Co-op hold all at baggage claim, he gathered with the new recruits in the terminal building expecting to be greeted by someone. Instead…nothing…no one. David went outside and was met with scorching heat and brilliant sunshine.

He saw an apparition standing by the wall, wearing a starched khaki safari suit, highly polished leather boots, leggings, belt and brace, which is similar to a Sam Browne but with the leather cross brace going through the left epaulet rather than the right, shining brass buttons, buckle and epaulets, and a stiff blue and khaki peaked cap.

He had a short haircut, golden brown complexion and was clean shaven. He did not move and didn't look very friendly. There were three brass chevrons on his sleeve.

When asked if he was there to greet the new recruits (which probably took the form of a Cockney 'Excuse me, mate'), he sprang to life. Waving a leather-bound swagger stick, he began shouting that they should all take their belongings over to a five-ton Bedford truck parked nearby, climb up the sides and roll up the loose canvas that was hanging from the roof. Again, not very friendly.

David, wearing new, highly fashionable and newly polished winklepicker shoes bought specially for the occasion, looked dubiously at his companions, shrugged and they began to clamber up the sides of the truck. His winklepickers, with their long pointed toes, didn't adapt well to climbing up the side of trucks and in hindsight David concedes that they were ridiculous.

The tarpaulins were rolled up to reveal a siding of stout wire mesh with holes spaced about every four feet. David thought this strange but got on with the task of loading his gear, whereupon everyone climbed over the back of the truck with their luggage and sat on the wooden benches positioned either side.

The apparition, whose three small brass chevrons on his sleeve obviously identified him as a police sergeant, drove the Bedford like a maniac, causing passengers and luggage to fly from one side of the truck to the other.

One of the new recruits, an Irishman, who later became known to his squad mates as Paddy Finn, looking wide-eyed and gormless, was heard to exclaim as he rolled his eyes skyward, "What the fuck have I let myself in for?"

When the vehicle finally came to rest, the recruits disembarked at a two-story red brick building and were hustled into a large office where a staff officer wearing a similar garb to their sergeant but with a crown on each epaulet and a Sam Browne, handed each recruit a document to sign, a document agreeing to serve the Crown for the prescribed three years as a constable in the British South Africa Police.

From a place that was later determined to be Police General Headquarters or PGHQ, the truck headed in the same chaotic fashion to the BSAP training depot. The training depot, and much of the curriculum, was originally designed by the Royal Canadian Mounted Police in the early 20th century.

Upon arriving at a relatively modern two-story apartment block, they again disembarked and looking up at the first floor balcony saw a flock of nearly bald heads shouting a variety of ribald comments—"Here's more P.O.M.E.s" (a term borrowed from Australia that refers to the letters stenciled on the shirts of convicts identifying them as Prisoners of Mother England), along with snide remarks about a 'bedroom tan' and 'get your hair cut', which made no sense at the time, but the penny soon dropped. Their welcome committee was obviously members of the previous intake.

The sergeant who had met them at the airport turned out to be their squad instructor and they were designated as the Number Twelve Squad of 1962.

In addition to the fourteen British recruits that David had flown out with, Twelve Squad was joined by three Rhodesians and two South Africans, bringing the total complement of Twelve Squad to 20. Each recruit was given a comfortable room in what was called Stopp's Hostel and was furnished with a bed, desk, chair and closet and David was quite impressed.

The building was obviously quite new, bathroom facilities were clean and modern and in fact it was quite an improvement over his previous accommodation on Bloemfontein Road.

The days passed very quickly. Kit, comprising summer and winter dress, dark blue riot kit with a white helmet, jodhpurs, white singlet and shorts and white plimsolls called tackies were issued along with a leather belt and brace, boots, gas mask and much, much more, all wrapped in a rough brown police blanket.

The next stop was at the police tailor and the saddler for their uniforms and leather accoutrements to be properly fitted.

While their uniforms were being made ready, they were transported to a local barber where, under the direction of their squad sergeant, David's carefully groomed hair was all but totally removed.

Very early morning wake-up calls were the norm and each recruit was given a horse to groom. David had never touched a horse before and the closest he'd ever been to one was the coalman's cart horse delivering coal to Bloemfontein Road during the winter months.

David's horse was a large, Roman-nosed and rather docile chestnut named Warlord and he adapted well to David's amateur ministrations with an assortment of brushes, curry combs and other paraphernalia associated with his daily grooming.

One surprise that David was totally unprepared for was that each recruit was required to employ a batman. Usually, one batman was shared between three recruits and their job was to wash, starch, iron and polish the various items of uniform that would be worn for the next six months. David's batman, he soon came to realize, would make the difference between progressing through the training depot relatively unscathed and living in constant torment.

Equitation occupied the early part of every day and the recruits were taught how to saddle, mount and ride their horse as well as how to groom and take care of it when out in the bush far from any farrier or veterinarian. One lesson learned was that when sponging the horse's mouth, nostrils and dock (anus), they were to be cleansed in that order. To do it backward would inevitably result in a painful bite or kick.

Another lesson learned was how to treat a horse with colic. The farrier assembled them behind a tethered horse and secured the horse's head high so that the front hooves were barely touching the ground and, therefore, it could not kick with its back legs.

The farrier then commenced to demonstrate how to perform a back rake. Firstly, you roll up your sleeve or better still take your shirt off; secondly, you remove your wristwatch, rings, etc. and smear your arm with grease; and thirdly, you insert hand, wrist, forearm and elbow as far into the horse's rectum as you can reach.

After cupping your hand, you withdraw the arm rapidly, covering all the attentive recruits in shit. This was followed by howls of laughter from the farrier.

David's first day of actually mounting and riding Warlord took place about two weeks into his training. The depot had two riding schools, which were basically sandy paddocks surrounded by tall wicker fences.

Having mounted their horses at the stables, the 20 recruits of the Number Twelve Squad walked their horses in single file to one of the riding schools. It should be noted that their horses took no notice of their riders' 'click-clicks' and 'giddy-ups' but reacted perfectly to the instructor's commands of 'walk on'.

Once inside the riding school, the horses formed a circle facing inwards toward the instructor. On the command 'walk on' they turned to the right and walked sedately in a counter-clockwise direction. On the command 'trrrot' they picked up a little speed, their riders began bouncing and two or three immediately fell off.

Chaos descended on the riding school. The horses continued to trot, riders who fell, scrambled to avoid sharp hooves. The instructor screamed obscenities at everyone and eventually order was restored.

Those members of the squad who managed to remain in their saddles were told to dismount and the entire squad was told that the following morning's equitation would be comprised of riding their mounts with no saddles, just a blanket secured by a wide strap that runs over the back and under the belly of the horse and called a surcingle.

It transpired that this was standard punishment for poor performance and was experienced on many, many occasions and for those uninformed readers, the surcingle and blanket was for the horse's benefit, not the riders. No stirrups meant nowhere to put your feet and that resulted in many involuntary dismounts!

As their horsemanship improved, they were allocated different horses and smarter horses that responded to a touch rather than to the instructors' voice commands.

David progressed from Warlord to Wayward, who refused to jump even the smallest hurdle, to Sandhurst, an ex-racehorse with a miserable temper and a tendency to kick and bite, but who was very fast, to Rajput, a magnificent horse who unfortunately was injured just prior to pass out and finally to Jasper, the best horse of all.

As their horsemanship improved, they were sometimes taken out onto the dry *vlei* or open area of ground, where they could progress from walk to trot, to canter, and finally to a full-blown gallop. David's first experience of riding a horse at the gallop was exhilarating beyond belief and a memory that he would forever cherish.

Compared to the trot or canter, the gallop was pure powerful delight. David felt his horse surge forward, doubling its speed into a smooth breath-taking motion and he could sense its sheer muscular power as he gave the horse its head. The adrenaline rush as he galloped alongside nineteen other horses was absolutely unforgettable.

The only difficulty was getting the animal to stop and he well remembers one squad member disappearing into the distance only to return to the depot hours later, leading his horse by the reigns as he walked beside it, completely chagrined.

Foot drill and arms drill was also a large part of the routine along with musketry, physical training, classroom instruction on Roman Dutch law and first aid, which included the provision of a mysterious maternity kit consisting of a small tin box containing one razor blade and two pieces of string.

For those uninitiated to the skills of childbirth, the two pieces of string were to tie the umbilical cord in two places about six inches apart and the razor blade to cut the cord between them. Quite simple, really!

Musketry comprised many hours of practice at the police rifle range. The weapons consisted of a personally issued Lee Enfield .303 rifle that David felt quite sure was left over from World War II. There were Sterling submachine guns that constantly jammed, a new addition to the armory, an Israeli Uzi submachine gun, and Webley and Scott .38 and .45 revolvers, the latter for use in destroying horses and cattle when necessary.

There were also shotguns—a well-made and sturdy semi-automatic with a five-round magazine and some old and decrepit greener shotguns with a Martini Henri action and safety catch. Sometimes the gun fired when releasing the safety catch, so it was important, so the instructor said, to take aim before releasing the safety catch!

They also had typing lessons and some very interesting sessions discussing the history and geography of Southern Rhodesia and the background of the origins of the British South Africa Police (nothing to do with South Africa at all but part of the Cecil John Rhodes foray into central Africa in the late 19th century with his British South Africa Company—hence the name).

David sometimes considers some aspects of life in the BSAP to be similar to rumors he had heard of life in the French Foreign Legion. The police officers he encountered were from all corners of the British Commonwealth and included Frenchmen from Mauritius, New Zealanders, Australians and, of course, South Africans, Rhodesians and Brits from all parts of the British Isles.

They also included a few remittance men, who were invariably British and from good families but who had disgraced themselves in some form or other and were sent far away and paid a monthly or perhaps annual remittance to stay there!

The British recruits became tan, lost their fashionable haircuts and a month later they gave the next intake a similar welcome to their own.

By this time, everyone was accustomed to their squad mates and most acquired nicknames. There was Geordie, who of course came from Newcastle, Scottish Jock, Irish Paddy and Welsh Taffy. David became Dicky Bird and for his entire 20 years in Africa, the name stuck. The name David became foreign, even to him, and he was to remain Dicky, or sometimes Dick, for good, or so it seemed.

Within a month of their arrival, Dick, as he was now known, and three fellow squad mates pooled their resources and purchased a huge 1939 black Packard sedan (which was originally the official vehicle of the Governor General of the Federation of Rhodesia and Nyasaland) for the princely sum of 50 pounds. Their smooth-running ride with a straight six-cylinder engine ate up the miles and the petrol but was the envy of the depot.

After a month of living in the relative luxury of Stopp's Hostel, Dick and his entire squad were moved to more austere quarters made of brick and timber, probably the original recruit quarters at the beginning of the century.

They were constantly warned by their instructors and the rather effeminate sergeant who taught first aid and was referred to behind his back as Sister Sunshine that on no account were they to fraternize with the ladies of the night, invariably Black or colored, as they were riddled with venereal disease.

Dick hadn't been in the depot very long when Sergeant Whitehead came looking for him and his squad mate Geordie. The sergeant, obviously scouting for potential rowers for the police rowing club, crammed the two of them into his immaculate MG sports car and took them off to a local drive-in restaurant for a bite to eat.

By the end of their outing, they had become members of the police rowing team and discovered that the police had a small boat club at Lake McIlwaine, about 30 miles from Salisbury, where there were two rowing clubs. Hunyani and the BSAP, with the latter housing two newly purchased and immaculate German-made fine coxed fours and not many policemen to row them.

Dick and Geordie, a rower from Newcastle on Tyne, were soon added to the BSAP rowing team and participated in several regattas in both Southern and Northern Rhodesia (now Zambia) and in one memorable race in Lourenço Marques (now Maputo) in Mozambique. They enjoyed rowing in the police crews and were permitted time off for training on Lake McIlwaine, much to the chagrin of their fellow police officers.

***

The rowing event in Mozambique deserves mention, although it occurred approximately a year or two after Dick's first introduction to the club.

A rather perplexed police superintendent met with Dick, who had become secretary of the police rowing club, and showed him a letter written in English from the police authorities in Lourenço Marques, which was the capital of Portuguese East Africa or Mozambique at that time.

Written in very poor English, the letter advised that a rowing race was being planned on the ocean alongside the esplanade at the upcoming traditional Naval Day festivities. The letter was very specific, stating that they would be honored if a BSAP crew would participate. Boats, accommodation and transportation would be provided.

The race would comprise a crew from the Mozambique police force and a crew from a private yacht club—Club Navale. The most amusing part of the letter stated that the racecourse would be with cocks a mile long!

This was taken to mean that each boat would have a coxswain (commonly referred to as the cox) and that the distance of the race would be one mile. At least this is hopefully what they meant; otherwise, the BSAP crew certainly wouldn't qualify!

It was agreed that four police oarsmen would attend, along with a coxswain and a police superintendent, presumably to keep order.

When it was time to leave Salisbury, the crew of four, which included Dick, boarded the train to Bulawayo, spent the night in police accommodations and boarded an overnight train to Lourenço Marques. Dick will never forget the train from Salisbury to Bulawayo, in particular the dining car.

It was absolutely magnificent and spoke of another age. Beautifully crafted cabinet work, soft lighting and lamp shades at every table. It reminded him of the films he had seen of the Orient Express.

Before leaving Bulawayo the following day, they spent the morning exercising at the police sports ground. Dick clearly remembers completing four laps of the track, or one mile, in just under six minutes and was not impressed with his performance.

They were met in Lourenço Marques by a well-spoken plain clothes police officer named Julio, who was to become their translator and guide, and they were transported in a brand-new unmarked Land Rover to the officer's mess. Their accommodation was first class and the food excellent. Wine, beer and an abundance of Portuguese specialties were laid before them and they made the most of it.

They had one week to acclimatize themselves to the environment, to train in the boat and along the racecourse and to socialize with their rowing opponents.

The opposing Mozambique police crew were all large men, not particularly young and not at all fluent in English, but between some sign language and the help of their plain clothes interpreter and guide, everyone got along famously. There was quite a lot of beer drinking and singing involved and despite the language difficulty, things were working out very well.

The day after they arrived, they were taken approximately two miles on a ferry across a very choppy Delagoa Bay to an island out in the bay. Inside a beautiful boathouse reposed two immaculate tub fours, carbon copies of the boat David first learned to row back at the Furnivall Rowing Club in London.

They had taken their own BSAP oars with them from Salisbury, the blades painted in the BSAP colors of blue and old gold, so without much ado they launched a tub four, actually referred to as a Yol du Mere by the Portuguese and set off across the bay toward the Club Navale on the mainland.

None of the crew had ever rowed on the ocean and Dick was the only one to have rowed in a tub four. Their coxswain was a seventeen-year-old police cadet who looked terrified and their superintendent went back on the ferry.

After a somewhat hazardous crossing, they found their way to the rather prestigious Club Navale yacht club, shipped their oars and set the boat onto a rack.

The following few days flew by. A large part of each day was taken up with training, but there was time for some sightseeing, visiting the Lourenço Marques magnificent Catholic cathedral and the famous Polana Hotel.

Their opposing crew members insisted on taking them to some sleazy bars and night clubs and on one occasion, when visiting a pub on the waterfront, they were approached by a heavily made-up prostitute. They pointed to their seventeen-year-old cadet as a possible customer and roared their heads off as the poor kid tried to fend off her advances. All ended well and the merry crew returned to their quarters none the worse for wear.

On another evening, unaccompanied by their Portuguese competitors, who they all suspected of trying to regale them with too much food and drink in an effort to reduce them to fat, drunken slobs by the time race day arrived, the six of them went out alone.

Dressed in their police blazers and ties, they gained admittance to a British ship, the *City of York*, which was docked in Lourenço Marques before heading up the east coast of Africa and through the Suez Canal and the Mediterranean before arriving in Britain.

The City Line had several ships on this route and were combined cargo and passenger vessels. Catering to about 100 passengers, the *City of York*'s accommodation was first class and when the six Rhodesian policemen were seated in the lounge Dick was overawed by the sedate and quiet luxury around him.

They each ordered a glass of Worthington 'E', which was served in a delicate glass, something similar to a large wine glass and when Dick took his first sip, he knew that he had encountered a brew far superior to anything he had ever tasted before.

The normally boisterous group behaved admirably, spoke quietly and after demolishing a few pints of Worthington 'E' departed with gracious farewells to the accommodating crew.

On race day, a large crowd was gathered along the waterfront for the entire length of the race. The three crews lined up at the start, the starter's gun was fired and they were off. Dick, seated in the stroke seat and setting the pace, used their usual method of getting the boat moving by using four short strokes followed by 20 long, powerful strokes and then settling down to a steady rhythm.

They soon left the Club Navale boat in their wake but were still neck and neck with their police opponents when their coxswain began edging their boat toward them. Dick told his coxswain to hold his course, but the Portuguese boat edged closer still until their oars clashed. This would never happen in a civilized boat race, but the boats were now locked together with the Portuguese blades in the BSAP's laps and vice versa.

The boats stopped, there was much shouting and gesticulating and eventually the boats disentangled and the race continued. There was a great deal of cat calling and shouting from the spectators on the shoreline and although Dick and his crew attempted to overhaul their opponents, they were forced to accept second place, losing by one boat length.

Much was made of the Portuguese police crew at the award ceremony, where they were presented with a huge trophy. The BSAP crew had to settle for five tiny silver medals.

A somewhat disillusioned police crew returned to Salisbury to face criticism and abuse from their fellow rowers, but in retrospect, they had to admit that a fine time was had by all and that they had done their best.

Chapter Four

Returning to 1963, Dick, having become somewhat accustomed to Southern Rhodesia, its people and climate, realized that the living standards and the lifestyle in general were far higher than that which he had experienced in London. At 6,000 feet above sea level, the climate was hot but dry in summer and cool but comfortable in winter. Rainfall was moderate and farming and mining were the two main industries.

People of all races seemed to blend well together. Six million Africans, 250,000 Europeans, mainly of British extraction and a smattering of coloreds (mixed races) and East Indians.

After completing his six months of intensive training, Dick's squad was to perform two passing-out parades. The first mounted on horseback to demonstrate their horsemanship, the second, and in different uniform, on foot and with rifles at the slope, demonstrating their foot drill.

With training at the police depot complete, some of the newly trained recruits were posted to various locations across the country, while twelve of the squad, including Dick, remained in Salisbury to provide a mounted escort for the opening of the Federal Parliament.

This was an annual tradition and entailed escorting the Governor General from the Government House to the Federal Parliament building, the Federation being made up of Southern and Northern Rhodesia and Nyasaland.

The pomp and ceremony associated with this event was of a huge magnitude by African standards and entailed a full military band and contingents of the armed forces, with large crowds lining the route.

The BSAP contribution was the military band and a mounted escort led by a commissioned officer with sword drawn. The twelve mounted troopers were on magnificent horses with spit-polished harness and saddlery, each carrying a ten-foot lance with a fluttering BSAP regimental pennant colored blue and old gold in one hand and four reins attached to a port mouth reversible bit in the other.

The mounted policemen were themselves adorned in heavy cavalry twill breaches, green tunics, spit-polished boots, leggings, belt and brace, spit-polished leather gauntlets and a white blanco'd pith helmet complete with brass chin strap and spike. Blanco was a tinned paste and came in many colors. It was used by soldiers throughout the British Commonwealth since 1880 and was used by police recruits to brighten rifle slings, pith helmets and plimpsoles.

As one can imagine, the month between the passing-out ceremony at the police depot and the opening of parliament was one of intense preparation and practice, including a trial run in the busy African police training school to get the horses used to noisy crowds, bands and so forth.

Every morning started with grooming and saddling their mounts, followed by familiarization with handling the horse with four reins in the left hand and dealing with a ten-foot lance in the right. For training purposes, the practice lances were made of thick, heavy dowels, whereas the actual lances to be used were made of bamboo, but both types were tipped with sharp steel points.

Much of the practice was carried out in the riding school, with the horses trotting two abreast. On one occasion, with David and his horse Rajput being on the outside, Dick was frustrated when Rajput kept scraping along the wicker fence, obviously satisfying an itch on his hindquarter. Then, the inevitable happened.

Rajput scraped the fence and a branch that had crept through the fence caught on David's lance. The lance, being held at its base in a leather cup attached to the stirrup and by Dick's right hand some five feet higher, broke in two. Dick was now holding about six inches of lance below his hand and five feet of lance above it.

The lance slowly tipped forward, the point jabbing the horse in front, which, understandably, kicked back at Rajput. With horses kicking, riders tumbling and lances flying in all directions, it took some time for calm to be restored.

Nevertheless, the BSAP mounted escort was a success. On arrival at the parliament building, they formed up on the right of the parade as befitted the senior regiment, followed by the Rhodesian Light Infantry and the Rhodesian African Rifles. The horses behaved and stood patiently until the ceremony was over, whereupon they trotted in formation back to the training depot.

Once their mounted escort duties were concluded, Dick and his eleven colleagues were transferred to some old WWII barracks at Cranbourne, where they were taught to drive Land Rovers and ride BSA 650cc Gold Flash motorcycles.

This, in itself, was quite an experience. Land Rovers in those days, or at least the ones they were learning on, were manual gear shift, four-wheel drive with no synchromesh. Every gear shift, whether up or down, required a double declutch maneuver, and every signal was a hand signal. Training entailed driving through deep sand and mud, as well as through and over rough terrain, using a four-wheel drive where necessary.

All of the driving school recruits save one had no driving experience whatsoever, but through patient and detailed instruction, each recruit was taught the police method of driving as taught by the Metropolitan police in Hendon back in England—a method that Dick has adhered to religiously and has passed on to his three offspring and basically consists of driving defensively.

Always be prepared for other drivers to do the unexpected, stay alert and be conscious of your surroundings, and remember, it usually takes two drivers to cause an accident; it's caused contributory negligence.

The same type of approach was taken with motorcycle training but was more or less a trial-and-error exercise on how to ride, maintain and repair these magnificent machines, but fortunately Dick could call upon his experience with his TWN motor scooter to some extent. All the recruits, however, were somewhat puzzled, as it appeared that after six months of equitation, horses were being replaced with motorcycles!

***

At this point, it must be mentioned that Dick had become the half-owner of the Packard behemoth as the other two owners had been transferred out of the area. Dick and the designated driver co-owner were frequently in the habit of visiting local drinking establishments in the evening when finances permitted and on one momentous occasion, they chose to take six fellow driving school colleagues with them.

Upon winding up the evening's festivities, the merry revelers wended their way back to Cranbourne barracks. Dick, another colleague and the driver occupied the front of the vehicle with the other five in the back.

On the drive back to Cranbourne barracks, through some mysterious happenstance, their vehicle careened off the road into a wooded thicket and after demolishing a few trees came to a halt with steam rising from beneath the bonnet.

One fellow in the back was established to have suffered a broken leg, but otherwise there appeared to be no injuries. The injured party was conveyed to hospital by a kindly passing motorist, while the remainder decided to walk the rest of the way and say nothing to the hierarchy at the police driving school.

For those who may not be aware, 1939 Packards did not have seat belts and at the time of impact Dick's face met rather harshly with the steel dashboard of that sturdy Packard. Being well lubricated, he had no trouble falling asleep once arriving at the barracks, but when preparing his toilet in front of the mirror the following morning, he noted with some alarm that his four front teeth were either cracked, broken or completely missing.

He quickly donned his police uniform and appeared on parade with his colleagues from the previous evening. They were a sorry mess sporting an assortment of bruises, black eyes, cuts and scratches. The uniformed instructor took one look and went ballistic. Dick was duly sent to the dentist who, in the fullness of time, fitted him with four immaculate teeth, which he still has to this day.

***

Once training was completed, Dick was posted to the Salisbury Central police station, where he worked eight-hour shifts patrolling various areas of the city sans teeth. This, in itself, created several problems: talking being one, looking like an idiot another.

In due course, he was transferred to a small office where he was required to perform annotations to law books, take charge of the exhibit room and generally kept out of the public eye until his teeth arrived, which they thankfully did in June of 1963.

On a brighter note, Dick became very active in the police rowing club and won several trophies at regattas in Rhodesia and Zambia. This entitled him to several benefits, including time off for training and travel to various regatta venues.

One advantage of having no front teeth was that they provided a wonderful open airway when gasping for breath during training and when racing. It was during this period that he acquired his four new front teeth, but he still took them out whenever racing and tucked them into his sock.

Training on Lake McIlwaine presented several surprises, one being the close proximity of hippopotamuses, crocodiles and other wild game as the lake was inside a game reserve. The hippo, incidentally, takes more lives than all of Africa's other wildlife combined.

One occasion that Dick remembers fondly was when they were training on the lake in the very early morning. They had camped out at the BSAP Yacht Club for a week so that they could get in plenty of practice before the upcoming regatta. They were rowing alongside the shoreline on the far side of the lake in a thick morning mist.

It was quiet, peaceful and they were practicing 'sitting' or 'balancing' the boat', letting it run with blades feathered and off the water. They had just taken a few strokes and started the run when, over to their right, the mist began to rise as they glided past the shoreline and there was complete silence save for the gentle hiss as the boat slid through the smooth water.

A small group of sable antelope drinking from the lake didn't scatter and they weren't alarmed, and Dick's crew sat the boat perfectly. It is an image ingrained in Dick's memory and one that he will never forget.

The sable antelope is one of the most spectacular antelopes to be seen anywhere and was, and perhaps still is, the country's national animal. It stands almost as tall as a horse, has a magnificent bluish purple coat, a white blaze down either side of its head and a massive pair of scimitar horns that sweep over its shoulders toward its withers in a huge semi-circle.

On another occasion, when training on Lake McIlwaine, they had the privilege of having an Oxford Blue and Queens Councilor, then a resident and practicing solicitor in Salisbury, coxing and coaching them. It was late afternoon with a strong wind and very choppy water.

They were about a mile from shore and heading back toward the boathouse when the wind grew stronger, the waves grew higher and their boat began shipping water to an alarming degree.

It eventually became obvious that the boat was sinking, water was pouring over the gunwales and they were forced to 'abandon ship'. All five of them were now in crocodile and hippo-infested waters, almost a mile from shore, with a 44-foot boat barely remaining afloat, thanks to its two watertight compartments in the bow and stern.

It took the best part of an hour to swim the boat to shore, store it in the boathouse and repair to the Hunyani Hills Hotel where, still soaking wet and much to the consternation of the staff, they drowned their sorrows in the bar before heading back to town.

Dick loved Africa and he loved rowing. One memorable regatta was held on the Kafue River some 20 miles outside the Northern Rhodesian (or it may have been Zambian by then) capital city of Lusaka. The property was owned by an elderly gentleman who lived on his boat with his two African wives. The boat wasn't particularly big and, in many ways, resembled Humphrey Bogart's *African queen.*

Accommodation for the crews, who were made up of men from the Hunyani rowing club in Salisbury and clubs from the copper-belt towns of Ndola and Kitwe in the northwestern sector of Zambia, took the form of tents. Food was adequate, basically eggs and sausages for breakfast and a *braaivleis* (barbecue) for lunch and dinner.

Several hippos frequented the river, along with a few crocs, all of which had to be chased off with shotguns firing blanks. This was a far cry from Dick's introduction to rowing on the river Thames, where interference from a few Teddy Boys was totally insignificant by comparison.

The races were all Henley-style, with two boats in each race. Once the one-mile course was cleared of wildlife, the racing began. Each event was competitive and well administered, with the three categories being classified as either Maidens (novice crews with no more than twelve months of experience), Juniors (crews with over twelve month's experience but with no more than two Junior wins) or Seniors (crews who had won more than two Junior wins).

Dick's crew was entered in the Men's Junior event and after several heats won the trophy. In addition to the trophy, which had to be handed back a year later, each crew member was presented with an engraved pewter beer mug, which is still one of Dick's prized possessions to this very day.

Beer drinkers may be interested to note that a pewter beer mug will keep beer cooler than any glass, bottle or tin can. Perfect for beer consumption in Central Africa on a hot summer's day!

Once he had acquired four new front teeth but with still six weeks to go before his 19th birthday, Ray, a good friend of Dick's, took him on a blind date with him and his girlfriend Naomi to meet her friend Joyce. Dick found Joyce slim, tall and pretty and was immediately attracted to her.

Unfortunately, both girls lived in a girl's hostel called Harmony House, which had a strictly enforced lock-up time of 10.00 p.m. Consequently, having returned later than the 10.00 p.m. curfew, the girls were locked out and there was nothing for it but for the four of them to spend a night in the car. Thus, a new romance was born.

Dick's date had been born in England, but her parents emigrated to Southern Rhodesia shortly after World War II. Her father, formerly a carpenter and small-time farmer in England, soon found employment as an assistant manager on a 7,000-acre tobacco farm near Bindura, a small town about 65 miles from Salisbury.

The whole family was conversant in a language called Fanagalo, commonly referred to as kitchen kaffir, although this term, in deference to political correctness, is no longer used. Fanagolo is a form of pidgin English originally created in the South African gold mines as a language that all could converse in, be they Africans with a variety of languages, Afrikaans or English and it was widely used in Rhodesia.

Dick quickly bonded with Joyce's father, always referring to him as Mr. B, and was fascinated by his achievements, drive, energy and ambition. Within the space of fifteen years, he had progressed from being a carpenter living in temporary immigrant accommodation at Cranbourne barracks—yes, the very ones that housed David at driving school and during riot stand-by—to being the owner of the Condwelani tobacco farm.

Condwelani, which Dick believed to be a Shona word meaning something to do with happiness, was the name Mr. B gave to the farm after he bought the original 7,000 acres and sold half of it to help pay off the bank loan.

With several hundred acres planted with tobacco and maize, a large herd of cattle, a township of over 50 African farm workers with their wives and families, six dams stocked with fish and a newly built and beautiful farmhouse, Condwelani was the pride of the area.

As their relationship progressed, Dick and Joyce visited the farm as often as possible and Dick became a close friend and admirer of Mr. B, who became something of a father figure to the nineteen-year-old Londoner.

He will always consider the eleven years that he spent in the BSAP to be the most transformative period of his life. It taught him fortitude and gave him self-confidence and an independence that he had never before experienced, but events were pending that would force him to take an inner look at himself, where he had been and where he was going.

One thing he was certain of was that the relationship between him and Joyce would continue to flourish. Joyce was well into the second year of her four-year hairdressing apprenticeship and decided it was time to move out of Harmony House into an apartment in Salisbury's avenues.

She shared the apartment with an old school friend, Jean, whose boyfriend John was a frequent visitor. Consequently, the four became friends, went on many outings together and are still in contact to this day.

Back to the subject of rowing, Dick's crew later attended a regatta in the copper-belt town of Kitwe in the very north of Zambia and at the instigation of some of the locals, they were encouraged to attend a party north of the border in the town of Elisabethville in the Belgian Congo (since renamed Zaire and later the Democratic Republic of the Congo).

With some trepidation, for the Congo at that time was embroiled in a vicious war where Irishman 'Mad Mike' Hoare and his white mercenaries were fighting against the Simba rebels on behalf of the Republic of Congo (and incidentally with the support of the CIA), they threw caution to the wind and entered the Congo, went to the party which was a well-attended and wild affair, and returned to Kitwe slightly worse wear.

David was now living in a police hostel on Fife Avenue in Salisbury that housed some 30 or 40 police officers. He had decent accommodation, dining room and bar, and transportation to and from Salisbury's city center. It was at about this time that he was awakened by a colleague with the dreadful news that U.S. President John Kennedy had been assassinated.

Letters from Mom and Dad arrived regularly and David was always diligent in replying promptly. His Sidcup girlfriend also wrote regularly and David was busy considering how to break the news to her about Joyce when a

'Dear John' letter arrived telling him that on a recent trip to Billy Butlin's holiday camp in the Channel Islands, she had found a new boyfriend and that he was toast.

Chapter Five

Dick's first posting outside Salisbury Central was to Harare, at that time one of two large African townships servicing Salisbury. The police station policed not only the township, but also Salisbury's industrial sites. The police station operated on a 24-hour basis with an investigation section and a seasoned chief inspector at the helm.

Single men's quarters consisted of a two-story building housing a dozen or so police officers and contained a bar, canteen and a swimming pool and tennis court on the grounds. Housing was also provided for all African police and their families and the entire complex was surrounded by six-foot security fencing.

The bar at the single men's mess was named the Southern Cross in honor of the captain of a ship of the same name. He was the deceased husband of the lady who ran the mess. Dick had been living there for a year or so and got to know her quite well.

Unfortunately for her, she took a holiday to Hong Kong to visit her daughter. While she was away, the sergeant who took over her responsibilities discovered that she had been embezzling mess funds for several years. She was tipped off before flying home and decided to retire to Scotland instead.

The Southern Cross was not without incident. Several noteworthy bar fights occurred, although a general spirit of comradery and goodwill existed. The bar was tastefully decorated with a variety of memorabilia, including pieces of medieval armor and some rather spectacular swords.

Dick regrets one foolish incident in which he and a colleague, having imbued too many drinks, agreed to a swordfight. The sword play began quite tamely but soon heated up as one of the combatants tried to cleave the other over the head while standing on the bar. A wild swing at the other's ankles was thwarted when he jumped deftly over the swinging blade.

At this point, the volunteer barman for the night, having remained reasonably sober and realizing that things were getting out of hand, raised his hand and demanded that they desist.

Unfortunately, his hand connected with one of the swords, which severed his finger, left hanging by a piece of skin and bright red blood gushing out everywhere. The swordplay ended and the injured party was taken to the hospital where the finger was reattached.

His misery didn't end there for, although the injured party sportingly blamed his injury on a slip and fall while carrying a glass of water, he still had a finger that stuck straight out when he closed his fist.

The fellow in question would not be considered good looking at the best of times, but during an earlier incident in which one of his front teeth had been knocked out, he had been provided with a partial upper denture by the accommodating police dentist.

The poor fellow was due to fly back to England to visit his family the following week, so in appreciation of his good sportsmanship over the sword incident, the mess threw a party for him the evening before his departure.

At breakfast the following morning, just before leaving, he remarked on feeling a bit queasy and went to the toilet to throw up. When returning to the breakfast table, he smiled, saying he felt much better. Unbeknownst to him, but obvious to all his compatriots, he had upchucked his false tooth down the toilet.

It was never discovered how his family reacted to his strange appearance when he arrived home, but Dick was sure he would have come up with some entertaining explanation. His finger was eventually repaired to some degree through a complicated operation involving tendons and ligaments, but was never quite the same again.

Harare had two police substations, Matapi and Stoddart, both deep inside the township and with limited staffing. Fighting, particularly on a Saturday night after a day at the beer hall, was a common occurrence, usually over women, politics or tribalism, with knives, axes or *pangas* (machetes) being the weapons of choice.

Ambulance services were practically non-existent and it was usually left to the constable on duty to transport the injured parties to hospital. It therefore became customary to bring, carry or drag injured parties to the charge office, and once statements and complaints had been documented and there was a good collection of individuals awaiting attention, they were stuffed into the station's long wheel-based Land Rover and transported to hospital.

Dick can recall one night when the charge office was overflowing with individuals with a variety of complaints, ranging from assault to theft. He noticed an African man seated quietly on a bench with a huge axe wound on his head. Blood was flowing freely from the man's scalp, but he waited patiently for his turn to be heard. He was gently walked to the Land Rover and quickly transported to hospital.

Dick never ceased to be amazed at the injuries that could be sustained with such fortitude. A well-documented case in point was when an African was stabbed in the eye with an *assegai* (spear), the serrated metal point of which passed through the corner of the man's eye and protruded an inch or two out of the back of his head.

He instantly fled the scene and, holding the long wooden shaft of the *assegai* before him, ran six miles to a Catholic mission. The sisters at the mission managed to cut the wooden shaft from the head of the assegai before transporting him to the nearest hospital several hours away.

Incredibly, the hospital was able to remove the eight-inch metal spearhead, stitch him up and send him home. Dick's copy of the BSAP monthly magazine, *Outpost*, showed before and after photographs of the incident in question and reported that he had no after-effects other than slightly blurred vision in the affected eye.

Riots were commonplace in both the Harare and Southerton African townships and usually started with the political rallies held in the local football field. These riots generally took the form of the township's hooligans smashing up their own township, attacking schools, community halls, beer halls, shops and recreational facilities put there to improve their living standards. This made no sense to Dick and had very little impact on the white-occupied areas of the city.

Each police officer stationed anywhere in the greater Salisbury area was required to participate in riot stand-by duties on a rotational basis. This meant eight white police constables and eight African constables living in the Cranbourne barracks 24 hours a day for two weeks. Four Land Rovers with two European and two African police officers in each were equipped with batons, shields, tear and smoke (CS) gas, firearms, ammunition and flares.

Whenever a riot broke out, the riot stand-by Land Rovers and crews would attend, form up and quell the riot. Dick, recollecting the Bedford 5-ton truck that transported him from the airport when first arriving in the country, now realized what those holes were for every four feet in the heavy wire mesh siding. They were to accommodate tear gas guns or shotguns when under attack.

Rioters and the police both seemed to consider Saturday nights to be similar to a game of football. Sometimes you win and sometimes you lose. Rocks, bricks and bottles, particularly ones filled with petrol, more commonly known as Molotov cocktails, were the rioter's weapons of choice, while the police had the more sophisticated batons, shields and tear gas.

No one's feelings were really hurt and firearms rarely used. It is important at this point to explain that the BSAP was an unarmed police force, although each station had an armory where firearms could be drawn in exceptional circumstances.

Dick was stationed at Harare for over two years, much of which was a posting to the sub-station of Matapi. The Matapi area of the large Harare township was densely populated and contained several multi-story buildings with communal showers and toilets, which were occupied by working men who were either single or whose wives and families live at home in the tribal trust lands.

The area also contained many small houses known collectively as Old Bricks, which contained rows and rows of small brick houses for single families.

One night shift, he was on duty when a report came in of a suicide. He had barely turned nineteen at the time and had never seen a dead body, so with some trepidation, he loaded the body box onto the roof of the Land Rover and, with an African constable and a reluctant informant, he drove to the scene. A crowd had formed outside the small house and there was much ululating and tear shedding going on.

With torch in hand, he cautiously approached the door, gingerly pushed it slowly open and entered, shone the light around the unlit single room but could not see a body.

While searching the room, the door slowly swung closed behind him and when he turned around, he nearly jumped out of his skin for there, hanging on a hook behind the door was the corpse, held by a piece of electrical cord around his neck, tongue protruding and eyes bulging. No one seemed to know what caused the poor fellow's misery and suicide was quite rare among the African population.

Thinking back to his instructor in the depot, he remembered advice such as 'never look flustered', 'set an example' and 'remain calm and take control'. He sidled past the corpse and, with the aid of his African constable, removed the body box from the roof of the Land Rover. The corpse was unhooked, placed in the body box and the box returned to the roof.

The worst was yet to come, for the body had to be placed in the mortuary, which was not a happy place to be, especially in the early hours of the morning. The mortuary, a place he'd never been before, was cold and dismal with no one around.

He unlocked the door and entered. There were several large refrigerator doors and he opened the nearest to see the bottoms of several pairs of bare feet, each pair with a paper tag tied to one of its big toes but no empty trays on which to deposit the corpse.

A search of the other refrigerator doors eventually revealed an empty tray, but not before revealing an assortment of bodies—men, women and babies, Black, white and colored, in various stages of dress and decomposition, but all with one thing in common—they all had bare feet with toe tags attached.

It is interesting to note that in virtually every incident involving the dead body of an African, Dick found that the shoes and socks had been removed at the scene. Perhaps it was a custom, but he never discovered the reason.

Having completed the requisite toe tag and attached it to a big toe, Dick and his African constable loaded their corpse onto a tray and commenced rolling it into the fridge. When they were halfway there, the corpse began to sit up and belched. Both Dick and the A/C yelped and withdrew.

What had happened? Was he not dead after all? It slowly dawned on them that the man's wrist had caught on the roller and as they slid the tray into place, it caused the corpse to sit up, expelling air from the lungs as it did so.

While stationed at Matapi, Dick adjusted to the African mentality and understood them more and more the longer he saw and dealt with them. Granted, their living standards were very low, but from their point of view, the townships were not their home but merely a means to an end where they could find work, earn some money and thus support their family back home.

Every one of them had a tribal home far from the big cities. Their wives, offspring and family elders lived in a *kraal*, or small-holding, which consisted of several huts, some goats or sheep, probably a few cattle, chickens and some crops.

Although all the townships that Dick was aware of had electricity, fresh running water and sewage, some habits are hard to break. On one occasion, he was called to a scene where a dead baby had been buried. The area was actually a fairly small patch of earth where Africans used to go to defecate. It was something that they had been used to doing for ages past and thought nothing of it.

One particular man, having the urge to 'spend a penny', dropped his pants, squatted down, and while waiting for nature to take its course, began scratching around with a convenient stick, thinking that he had found a sweet potato.

The small protrusion appeared to have one of those little lumps that are common to sweet potatoes, but as he scratched deeper, he discovered that his sweet potato was actually a baby's foot and the little lump was a toe. At that point, he decided to notify the police.

Dick had never eaten a sweet potato at that point and since then has vowed that he never will.

Another sad moment occurred when Dick and a fellow police officer were called to an apparent carbon monoxide poisoning in the township. It was wintertime and could get very cold at night and upon their arrival, they found that the family occupying their small house had lit a fire inside to keep the family warm.

There was no fireplace and no chimney and when the old grandmother awoke, she found her daughter, son-in-law and all four children to be unconscious.

Dick found that the two youngest children, a baby and a toddler, were both deceased; a teenage boy and girl were unconscious and barely breathing and the parents groggy but awake. The grandmother was in fine fettle but inconsolable with grief.

He and his colleague loaded all but the grandmother into the Land Rover. She had obviously never ridden in a motor vehicle before and kicked up such a fuss that she was left behind while they transported everyone else to the hospital. It was later learned that the two teenagers had passed away, but the parents had made a full recovery.

David learned something that day for, certainly in that instance, the older you are, the better your body can deal with carbon monoxide poisoning.

***

Dick well remembers the late evenings at Matapi when the smell of wood smoke and the beat of African drums resonated throughout the area. One late evening, when on patrol in the Old Bricks area, he came upon a group of approximately 100 men and women holding a *shabeen* (party).

There were a few drummers beating out a rhythm on their traditional game skin drums, several men and women dancing on the bare earth between the houses and the remainder just onlookers, drinks in hand, laughing, talking and obviously having a good time.

Dick parked the police Land Rover behind the throng where he could have a good view of the proceedings and he and his African constable climbed onto the roof to watch. The participants were not at all intimidated or threatened by their presence; in fact, several of them raised a glass, or rather a small bucket, for this was the preferred beer container of choice, in welcome.

The *shabeen* became noisier and the dancers more uninhibited as the evening progressed and David clearly remembers one rather short, quite elderly and definitely overweight woman performing a somewhat erotic dance with her young male companion.

She turned her back to him, swaying and stomping in time with the drummers as she slowly sidled closer, eventually grinding her buttocks into him. Then, as he went to place his arms around her, she slowly withdrew, waggling a finger and laughing at him and then repeated the process all over again.

Another episode worth recounting, and Dick witnessed it on more than one occasion, was when, on Sunday mornings, small groups of colorfully dressed men, usually a dozen or so, would collect in a quiet area of bush to begin their religious ceremony. These men, known as apostolics, wore long robes and each carried a staff. They would form a circle and begin, accompanied by a drumbeat, to chant as they slowly began walking.

The walking soon became a trot and later they began leaping into the air every three or four steps. Their eyes became glazed as they became entranced, the pace quickened and the leaps became higher. This went on for over an hour and Dick never witnessed any speaking or sermon of any description.

It seemed to him that the whole purpose of the exercise was to transport the participants out of this world into something better. They didn't smoke anything in his presence; perhaps they had cottoned onto a new way of getting high without breaking any laws. It was also a great way to stay fit!

Chapter Six

A serious rift had occurred between Britain and Southern Rhodesia since Dick joined the Force in 1962 and in 1965, the Prime Minister of Southern Rhodesia, Ian Smith, and the governing Rhodesia Front Party were adamant that European rule must remain in force for the foreseeable future, whereas Britain's Labor government, led by Harold Wilson, was insisting on 'one man, one vote', meaning handing the country over to African rule.

Smith argued that the Africans were not competent to run the country and cited the many examples to the north where African rule ended in dictatorships, hunger and corruption. Wilson's response was that democracy must prevail and that the people of Rhodesia as a whole should decide on their future.

While this was going on, the two major African political parties, Z.A.P.U. (Zimbabwe African Peoples Union), led by Matabeleland's Joshua Nkomo, and Z.A.N.U. (Zimbabwe African Nationalist Union), led by Mashonaland's Robert Mugabe, were at loggerheads as to who should rule the country. Z.A.P.U. received limited backing from Russia while Z.A.N.U. received support from China.

Politics and tribalism are much of the same thing in Africa, and while Nkomo was a Matabele, an offshoot of the brave and warlike Zulu nation in South Africa, Mugabe was a Shona, a tribe native to Rhodesia and considered by the Matabele to be weak and inferior. The Shona, however, were far more numerous than the Matabele and when it came to election time, there was no doubt who would emerge as the winner.

This polarization of African politics created more unrest and rioting in the African townships and led to an influx of terrorism into Rhodesia. Northern Rhodesia and Nyasaland had both gained independence from Britain, becoming Zambia and Malawi, and Southern Rhodesia, now simply named Rhodesia, became more allied with South Africa and Portuguese East Africa, otherwise known as Mozambique.

Z.A.P.U. and Z.A.N.U. terrorists with training camps in Russia, China and Zambia became a serious threat attacking lonely farms, killing farmers and their families, and intimidating, torturing and killing farm workers and outlying tribesmen and women.

A typical example of terrorist intimidation tactics was when a group of 20 or so armed terrorists invaded a peaceful African *kraal*, or village, threatened them with death or mutilation if they cooperated with Rhodesian security forces.

To add force to their warning, they proceeded to tear off a young girl's lips with a pair of pliers—a sickening example of the terrorism that the country was dealing with.

Another example of the atrocities that these so-called freedom fighters performed was when, armed with a surface-to-air missile, they brought down a Rhodesian Airways turbo prop airliner that was full of tourists flying into Victoria Falls.

The pilot managed to bring the aircraft down in the bush close to the huge Wankie game reserve, with many survivors suffering only minor or no injuries. The terrorists quickly arrived on the scene and began murdering the survivors. Only one passenger, a Scandinavian tourist, managed to escape unseen into the bush and later reported what he had seen.

Several female passengers and two air hostesses were brutally and repeatedly raped before being slaughtered. He was the sole survivor. Needless to say, David's attitude toward terrorism was set, sealed and delivered.

Rhodesia's armed forces were more than a match for these poorly trained and, in some cases, juvenile terrorists, with Rhodesian forces sustaining a kill rate of much more than ten to one. Conscription was introduced in Rhodesia and the armed forces were considerably beefed up.

The BSAP created a Police Anti-Terrorist Unit (P.A.T.U.), which provided support to the armed forces, and their Second World War Lee Enfield .303 rifles were replaced with Belgian FN automatic and semi-automatic weapons.

Dick had received helicopter training and to this end he and a few other police officers, European and African, were taken to an airfield where one of the Rhodesian Air Force's small Allouette helicopters was waiting. The purpose of the training was to acclimatize them to the maneuverability of the helicopter and to experience jumping out while it hovered about six feet off the ground.

The Allouette had a pilot and co-pilot seated at the front and one bench seat behind them, which could hold four people. There were no doors and only small lap belts to hold the backseat passengers in place.

Dick and another constable sat on the outside, where the doors should have been, while two African constables sat between them, their shako helmets firmly placed on their heads. The cowboy piloting the helicopter thoroughly enjoyed himself, swinging the aircraft first to the left and then to the right, frightening the bejesus out of his backseat passengers.

Dick cast a glance at the African constable sitting beside him and noticed that his coloring had faded to an unhealthy gray, his lips had turned almost white and his eyes were as big as saucers. Then his helmet fell off, bounced across Dick's lap and went sailing off into the blue yonder.

When the helicopter returned to hover above the ground for the deplaning exercise, everyone was glad to bail out, regardless of whether it was six or 60 feet off the ground. Then, the African constable went to look for his helmet.

As the Z.A.P.U. and Z.A.N.U. terrorist threats grew, more and more incidents of terrorist atrocities were occurring. One example that sickened Dick was when, armed with the infamous Kalashnikov AK-47 automatic rifle, terrorists were killing African wildlife, no doubt for food, but in a most inhumane way.

Whereas an experienced hunter would carefully place his shot to limit the animals' suffering, these so-called freedom fighters would spray the animal with bullets and wait for it to die. Dick, already averse to hunting and animal cruelty, could only shake his head in horror, confusion and disbelief.

Prime Minister Ian Smith declared a Unilateral Declaration of Independence (U.D.I.) on 11 November 1965, severing Rhodesia's allegiance to the Crown and a state of emergency was declared. This was only the second incident of a U.D.I occurring anywhere in the world, the first being when the United States of America declared its secession from England in 1776.

Dick and his colleagues, most of whom were British, had been forewarned that this might occur and were generally supportive of the move. They had first-hand experience of Rhodesia's African population and, as did Dick, believed that they were incapable of governing the country, a belief that was admirably borne out by the subsequent election of Robert Mugabe and his catastrophic 37 years as either Prime Minister or President of Zimbabwe.

They were nonetheless disappointed that a diplomatic solution could not have been reached and were well aware of the consequences that a U.D.I. would produce in the Harare township.

Some British members of the force chose to desert and return to Britain, finding themselves unable to support the Smith government. Dick chose to stay.

Sure enough, riots broke out everywhere across the country and the police were hard pressed to control them. The police were also under increasing pressure to deal with growing incidents of property crime and crimes of violence and Dick can well remember taking many investigation dockets to Joyce's apartment to work on after hours.

***

An incident that had nothing to do with riots or terrorism was when Dick, now stationed back at the main Harare police station and the only white police officer on night duty, took pity on his African sergeant. The sergeant needed to cycle through the industrial sites, checking on several African constables who were walking or cycling their beats in different areas. The sergeant was suffering a serious case of gout and could hardly walk, let alone cycle, so Dick drove him around the site in the station's Land Rover.

It was a quiet, hot night and as they drove slowly through the streets and alleyways, they came across a young African man carrying a large box on his shoulder. They stopped and asked him where he was going at this hour and he explained that he had brought a box full of socks from Gwelo for his brother's shop but had missed the last bus.

The explanation seemed quite reasonable, and with nothing better to do and obviously suffering from a bout of simple mindedness, Dick offered to give him a lift to his brother's house, which was in the 'old bricks' neighborhood of Harare township and within their police area.

Loading the man and his box into the back of the Land Rover, they set off for 'old bricks', but upon arrival, their passenger seemed confused as to which house was his brother's. After a couple of stops and starts, the back door flew open and their passenger fled. Dick could have kicked himself for being such a sucker.

The sergeant with gout was no use, so Dick chased after the culprit, dodging through the houses, across dirt lanes and into a cemetery, keeping the man in sight despite very poor lighting. Eventually the culprit ran into a six-foot fence and while trying to scale it, Dick pulled him down and struggled with him.

The blows that Dick sustained were sharp and painful and he soon realized that they were from a knife, not a fist. Seeing that he was covered in blood and deciding that discretion was the better part of valor, he backed off.

He could hear his African sergeant blowing his police whistle, but not knowing the extent of his injuries, Dick returned to the Land Rover and drove the ten miles to Salisbury hospital. It was only there that he discovered that he had six stab wounds, including two in the neck and one over his heart, limited in depth due to the presence of a police notebook in his left breast pocket, which had been almost sliced in half.

When returning to the police station after getting stitched up, Dick was delighted to discover that his African sergeant, persisting with his whistle, had encountered an African police reserve patrol and they had succeeded in arresting the culprit. It turned out that the miserable offender, a lad of about seventeen, had broken into a warehouse in the town of Gwelo and had stolen the box of socks.

Surprise, surprise—there was no brother and no shop. The offender was subsequently sentenced to six months in jail for housebreaking, theft and assault with the intent to cause grievous bodily harm.

That was definitely one incident that would not find its way into Mom and Dad's monthly letter, but it certainly made a difference to Dick's way of thinking. Up until that point, he took the deference and respect with which Africans treated the police for granted, probably thinking that it was because he was white.

This was truly his first experience of an intimate, one-on-one confrontation with an African and it instilled in him the never-before recognition that he was not bulletproof and he had better be more careful in future. A lesson well learned.

Dick and Joyce were planning to marry in May 1966, and on one bright and sunny November morning, with only six months to go, Dick, being off-duty and in civilian clothes, had arranged to meet Joyce for lunch in Salisbury's city center.

They were casually walking along Gordon Avenue; the town was full of people of all races going about their daily business when Dick observed a group of about a dozen African men walking toward them, occupying the entire breadth of the sidewalk. They were forcing people out of their way and obviously intent on causing trouble.

One gentleman, just ahead of them and obviously unaware of the trouble that was heading his way, was preoccupied gazing into a jeweler's shop window when, as the group reached him, they descended on him like a pack of dogs, kicking and punching him as he curled up and tried to protect himself.

Without thinking, Dick flew into a rage and attacked the group, which surprisingly broke up and fled in all directions. He gave chase to one individual, through downtown traffic and across intersections, until the man he was pursuing ran into the open doorway of a millinery shop with Dick in hot pursuit and the shop assistant gaping in horror.

As the villain tried to escape via the shop's back door, Dick tackled him and restrained him until a police car arrived and took the culprit away. Dick eventually located his thoroughly bewildered fiancée back at her hairdressing salon and had some difficulty explaining why he had left her in such a dangerous situation.

Trying to rationalize his behavior to himself, he could only conclude that he had reacted before thinking, which, in Dick's case tended to be a frequent occurrence. Fortunately, things turned out well and at least one troublemaker were taken off the streets for a while.

When meeting the window shopper some weeks later, there was no word of thanks. Just a 'Well, I suppose you were just doing your job, mate'. Some people!

***

Among Dick's associates in the BSAP, one individual stationed with him at Harare deserves special mention. He was a good bit older than Dick, corpulent of build and a 'great white hunter' to the core.

He was a well-educated Englishman who wrote many articles on the subject of big game hunting in Africa, mostly for American gun magazines and periodicals.

On one occasion, he took two Americans on safari and Dick remembers their arrival in Salisbury since they were accommodated in the Harare police mess.

The two gentlemen, one middle-aged and the other somewhat older, arrived with expensive-looking luggage and their hunting rifles in beautifully made rifle cases. Dick and his colleagues became somewhat perturbed, knowing that their 'big white hunter' was something of a loose cannon. He was sloppy when out of uniform and rather disorganized.

In fact, he had been promoted to sergeant twice and demoted twice. Had these gentlemen really known what they were letting themselves in for?

They stayed for a couple of nights before heading out, had plenty of money and insisted on buying round after round of drinks, which guaranteed a well patronized bar.

On the morning of their departure on safari, their esteemed leader turned up with one of his pals and two Land Rovers, one a pink open-topped job and the other a more conventional khaki that was towing a large trailer.

They were equipped with expensive permits issued by the game department, which allowed them to kill several game animals, including elephants. The Land Rovers were full of camping equipment and provisions and they expected to be gone for two weeks.

Things quietened down at the mess and returned to normal for a few days. Then the younger of the two Americans turned up alone, clutching his hunting rifle in its expensive case and a few belongings in a plastic bag. When asked why he had returned so early, his response was fairly noncommittal, saying that he didn't enjoy his safari and was returning home.

He came into the bar, joined by a few off-duty police officers, but pretty much avoided questions regarding his early return. He then had the audacity to ask one of the men, bearing in mind that they were all police officers, if they could find him a prostitute for the night. He soon sat, alone and despondent, in the bar and caught a flight back to the US in the morning.

Some ten days later, Dick was seated on the upstairs balcony of the police mess when, in the distance, he saw a very dark cloud appear on the horizon. As it came closer on the highway, he saw that it was the two Land Rovers returning from their safari with a huge cloud of flies hovering above them.

Running down to greet them as they pulled into the parking lot, he was overwhelmed by the stink of putrefying meat and saw several skins, hides, heads and elephant feet piled in the trailer. The three hunters, stinking almost as much as their cargo, announced that their safari had been a huge success and hurried inside for a shower, shave and clean up.

Later, when gathering in the bar, the American chap was overflowing with delight as he described their adventures and the other two, while enjoying their first cold beer in two weeks, remained rather morose and quiet. When asked about their American colleague who had left early, they just changed the subject, but Dick later learned that the poor fellow, overcome by excitement when he saw his first elephant, shot it dead.

It was a young elephant, not yet mature and with small tusks, certainly not a prize worth taking. Furthermore, to shoot an elephant that young was criminally and morally wrong and wasted one of their two permits for elephant kills.

Apparently, in absolute disgust at the shooting, the elephant killer was taken to a dirt road where an African bus, usually loaded with people, goats and chickens, would at some point arrive. He was told to return to Harare, pack his bags and leave, banished from the safari.

The morning following the return of the great white hunters, Dick went into one of the bathrooms for a shower and was horrified to find a complete buffalo hide soaking in the bathtub and stinking to high heaven.

"We're just trying to clean it up a bit by soaking it in salt water," came the excuse from the 'loose cannon' referred to earlier.

Dick had never been and still isn't a fan of game hunting, but he recognized that most hunters are good conservationists with probably more empathy for the game they hunt than the average man in the street.

Culling is necessary in Africa, especially elephants, as the damage they cause to trees and undergrowth is to the detriment of the many other species that live in the wild with them.

As an aside, Dick's great white hunter pal was bitten on the finger by a poisonous snake, either a green or black mamba, on a later hunt. With only seconds to act, he withdrew his hunting knife and amputated his own finger.

It was not long after that that he passed away—a colorful man with a colorful past who ate too much, drank too much, but lived life to the fullest.

***

Meanwhile, wedding preparations were well underway. Mr. and Mrs. B had booked a large room at the Park Lane Hotel and approximately 100 guests had been invited. Several farmers and their families from the Bindura area, several police officers and many friends from outlying areas attended. The ceremony was held in Salisbury's police chapel.

The bride, looking radiant in a beautiful white wedding dress and Dick in his full ceremonial uniform, were duly wed and, when leaving the chapel, were showered with confetti and rice as they walked beneath an archway of glistening bayonets presented by a police guard of honor.

Formalities concluded, the bride and groom departed in their newly acquired Volvo 122S saloon heading for a six-week honeymoon at Plettenberg Bay on the famous Garden Route 200 miles northeast of Cape Town. The beautiful oceanfront apartment they occupied, called Roberg View, was owned by Mr. and Mrs. B and generously donated as part of their wedding gift.

A wonderful honeymoon followed, with walks on the beach, a week-long visit to friends in Cape Town, and many other exciting experiences, one of which was to add another dimension to Dick's life. It occurred one night when, probably around two in the morning, Dick couldn't sleep, so he got up and made a cup of tea.

He'd been thinking about the year he had spent studying art and interior design and had an irresistible urge to paint or draw something. There were no art supplies at hand, but he found some paper and a pencil and began sketching a bunch of flowers standing on the coffee table.

When his new bride awoke, she found him still hard at it and at that moment he decided that he would take up art as a pastime. He was now 22, over four years after leaving college, but realized that he still had the desire, the instinct and the ability to draw and paint.

Chapter Seven

With the honeymoon over, the newlyweds returned to Salisbury, where they rented a townhouse. Mr. B had sold the farm and moved to Louis Trichardt in South Africa's Northern Transvaal, and the newlyweds acquired Roger, the family dog, a beautiful long-haired German Shepherd.

Joyce, who had now completed her four-year hairdressing apprenticeship, soon became pregnant. Dick sat his sergeant's exam and passed with flying colors. He had been transferred to the European suburb of Rhodesville, and while seconded to provide security at a terrorist trial at Rhodesia's High Court, he received a message from home.

The baby was coming and his wife needed taking to hospital. Dick was relieved of his duties for one hour, tore home with a police car leading the way, complete with flashing blue light and siren blaring, and conveyed the tearful and hesitant mother-to-be to hospital, where he assured the hospital staff that he would return as soon as the High Court proceedings had ended, a matter of two hours at most.

He reluctantly returned to duty. When he made his way back to the hospital at about 4:30 pm, he was presented with a baby boy who'd arrived miraculously just minutes after he had left the hospital.

It was decided to name their son Sean, probably because of the current popularity of the James Bond hero Sean Connery. Sean was a healthy, bouncy baby who gave the couple much pleasure and pride and fitted in well with the now-growing Bird family.

Dick, upon acquiring his sergeant's stripes, was transferred back to Salisbury Central, this time to license inspectors and eventually headed up the drug and vice section. The license inspector unit was divided into two departments.

The plain clothes drug and vice section which primarily dealt with marijuana, known locally by the Afrikaans word dagga, and prostitution while the uniformed section oversaw restaurants and bars, ensuring that they remained in compliance with their permits and licenses. The entire unit was headed by a police inspector who administered rather than participated in the unit's activities.

In an effort to transform the BSAP into a less racist entity, African constables and African sergeants were now just referred to as Constables and Sergeants and the former Constables and Sergeants became Patrol Officers and Section Officers.

Dick and three plain clothes patrol officers addressed the growing drug problem in the city, which included speaking at schools on the dangers of drugs. The information made available to them at that time, and which was common knowledge throughout the world, was that marijuana (known by a variety of names including pot, grass, hashish and cannabis) was harmful, addictive and likely to lead the user into using more potent drugs.

It is confusing to him that today we are being told the exact opposite. Were all his efforts in vain or is the world just capitulating to the inevitable?

He was also required to visit local strip clubs to ensure that the performers abided by the laws relating to G-strings and nipple caps—another constraint that has fallen by the wayside. This was a hardship that no one objected to, and David often reflects on the antics of the Tantalizing Tassel Tosser and of Nadya of the Nile, the latter who in actual fact came from the small Rhodesian town of Que-Que!

It may interest some to note that the Tantalizing Tassel Tosser was indeed quite talented. Having four tassels, two attached to her nipples and two to the cheeks of her bottom, she would call out, as if starting a four-engine aircraft, 'fire one' and just one tassel would begin to twirl, 'fire two' and a second would twirl, and so forth until all four tassels were spinning furiously.

Then, at a loud roll from the drummer, all four tassels would stop and begin spinning in the opposite direction. Absolutely fascinating.

Dick and his merry men were also required to control prostitution, which in Salisbury basically amounted to African female streetwalkers. This involved conducting periodic traps in the form of a white plain clothes officer in a civilian car assuming the role of a potential client, while three or four colleagues followed at a discrete distance.

Once the prostitute had climbed into the car and discussed terms for her services, a flash of the brake lights alerted the occupants in the following vehicle who then pulled them over, identified themselves as police officers and arrested the culprit. It was very important that the tailing occupants kept a close watch on their colleague's vehicle.

The system worked perfectly time after time, until the license inspector decided that he should fill the role of the client. A middle-aged Scotsman in civilian clothes and driving his wife's Peugeot was the perfect trap and before long he was seen to pull over beside a shapely African woman clad in the smallest of mini-skirts and not much else. A brief encounter ensued, following which she jumped into the Peugeot and they were off.

The inspector's car turned into an area generally known as the cow's guts and performed a confusing series of left and right turns but no flashing brake lights. The tailing car, another civilian vehicle of dubious vintage, was having difficulty keeping the Peugeot in sight, and with stop signs and civilian crosswalks to contend with, they lost their inspector.

A frantic search began of all the known brothels in the area and eventually the inspector's Peugeot was located—but empty! While Dick stood nonplussed on the sidewalk calling out for his inspector, a plaintive cry of 'Help—I'm down here' was heard.

He was eventually discovered, stripped down to his underpants with the prostitute naked and about to pounce. Presumably caught up in the excitement of the moment, the inspector admitted that he had totally forgotten to flash his brake lights and was waiting desperately for his men to pull him over.

Needless to say, no prosecution was forthcoming and there were no more prostitute traps for the inspector in charge.

These forays into the world of vice and drugs did not go over very well with Dick's wife Joyce and resulted in a brief separation.

Due to the stress placed on their marriage, Dick decided to request a transfer out of Salisbury and was posted to Umtali, a scenic resort town in the eastern highlands on the border with Mozambique. They rented a new townhouse apartment in a small complex named Park Vista, which had a swimming pool and a few other amenities.

With only 10 apartments, it was quiet and rather refined. Roger adapted well to his new home but was now getting old with severe arthritis in his back legs. One-year-old Sean was growing fast and his mother was enjoying the role of a stay-at-home mom.

Dick, now back in uniform, drew duty as a charge office section officer and dealt with the usual spate of property crimes, violence and drunkenness.

An amusing event worth relating is an evening when he was on night shift. The only patrol officer on duty with him was a rather intelligent fellow with absolutely no common sense. Dick had found this to be the case quite often and frequently considers this failure applies to the antics of many politicians.

A call had come in regarding an African woman lying drunk in the gutter outside a popular drinking establishment. Dick dispatched his patrol officer, who took the station's newly acquired Mini-Moke instead of the Land Rover. The Mini-Moke was an Austin Mini with no top and a bench seat in the back, somewhat similar to a beach buggy.

Shortly afterwards, the patrol officer returned in the Mini-Moke.

"Where's the woman?" Dick asked.

"I don't know," he replied. "I put her on the bench seat behind me but when I got here, she was gone."

Knowing this particular patrol officer's inclination to drive rather erratically, Dick realized that the woman had probably slid off the bench seat and told him to take the Land Rover, find the woman and bring her to the station. Shortly thereafter, a slightly worse for wear and totally drunk woman was locked up for the night and a suitably chastised patrol officer informed that he was no longer allowed to drive the Mini-Moke.

At around this time, Dick was instructed to take several constables out to a disused quarry to teach them how to use the greener shotgun—the one with the Martini Henri action and dodgy safety release. This was before some bright spark had the idea of supplying ear protectors while on the range.

During the course of his day of training, the 10 constables, who had never before used any type of firearm, Dick had some quite harrowing experiences. One man, having loaded his shotgun while his comrades fired their twelve bores at the metal plates being used as targets, was experiencing some difficulty.

Dick froze in horror as the man first looked down the barrel and then banged its butt on the ground before pointing it at Dick, saying, "Sir, I pulled the trigger, but nothing happened."

At that point, Dick saw him notice the safety catch and as he released it, Dick dived for cover. Fortunately, the gun didn't discharge. Everyone was told to unload and put their weapons down whereupon he repeated once more how to load, aim, release the safety catch, then pull the trigger and to never, never point their weapon at anyone unless they intended to shoot them.

At the end of his day at the quarry, Dick was stone deaf, save for a persistent ringing in his ears. When he later consulted an ear specialist, he was told that although the tinnitus would eventually dissipate, his hearing would always be impaired to some degree. False teeth, half deaf, what was next?

***

Back at Park Vista, Roger's condition deteriorated to the point where he had to be put down and this was a tragedy for the whole family. However, a puppy soon arrived on the scene: a German Shepherd/Collie with a few other breeds mixed in who was named Scamp. Sean and Scamp quickly became friends and remained friends for many years thereafter.

On one trip down to Louis Trichardt from Umtali to visit Mr. and Mrs. B, by this time traveling in an Austin Mini, having down-graded their beautiful Volvo 122S some time ago for a Ford Cortina station wagon and then to the Mini, they were traveling south along the strip road between Fort Victoria and Beitbridge when their little Mini suddenly stopped.

A strip road is basically a dirt road with two strips of tar spaced wide enough apart for a car's wheel to run on, similar to railroad tracks. If a vehicle approached from the opposite direction, each vehicle moved over to the left so that its left wheels ran on the dirt, while the right wheels ran on the left-hand strip.

Dick was (and still is) no mechanic and, after desperately messing with spark plugs, distributer and carburettor for a few minutes, realized that he was out of his depth. He decided to wait for another motorist to arrive and request assistance and after 30 minutes or so, a young couple arrived.

They were no use in discovering what was wrong with the Mini but offered to take Joyce and Sean to Beitbridge, a distance of over 100 miles and drop them off at the Beitbridge hotel to await Dick's arrival.

Once they had departed, Dick sat in the middle of nowhere, waiting for another motorist to arrive in the hope that it would be someone who could assist in getting the car started. If that failed, he would have to cadge a lift to Beitbridge himself and arrange for a tow truck to bring the Mini in for repairs.

At the time, it didn't seem too much of an ordeal, but thinking back, with no sounds other than a few insects and miles from any form of habitation and with an abundant source of wildlife and possibly terrorists in all directions, it was probably not the safest of locations to break down.

About 30 minutes later, two vehicles arrived containing two Italian families who had driven down from Zambia on their way to Durban. Incredibly, both men were motor mechanics and told Dick to step aside. They produced all kinds of jacks and tools, crawled beneath the Mini and declared that the problem had been discovered.

Back then, the Mini had its twelve-volt battery housed in the boot, not the engine compartment, and a cable ran beneath the car from the boot to the engine. A stone or rock from the dirt road had broken the cable and the two mechanics set about repairing it.

Meanwhile, their wives were fussing around Dick, offering him sandwiches, cakes and biscuits, which he declined. He did, however, gratefully accept an orange juice, produced fresh and cold from their ice-filled cooler. The orange juice was like something he had never seen before.

It was contained in a plastic orange, which one of the ladies proudly presented and cut off the tip, indicating that he should tip his head back, squeeze the orange and pour the juice down his throat. He followed her instructions to a T, except that the juice went down his windpipe instead of his throat.

What followed was ridiculous. Dick couldn't breathe and began choking, collapsing on his hands and knees and thinking that he might be the first person ever to have drowned in orange juice. The women began shouting and one of their husbands banged his head as he struggled from beneath the Mini to see what all the fuss was about.

Eventually, calm was restored, Dick began to breathe, the Mini was repaired and the good Samaritans continued on their way to Durban. Dick picked up his family at the Beitbridge hotel and eventually arrived at Mr. and Mrs. B's house later than anticipated, but with a tale to tell.

***

Shortly afterwards, Dick was posted to the Sakubva police station, a small satellite station in the local African township. The police station was situated on a two-acre parcel of land lovingly landscaped by the inspector in charge, aided and abetted by their Nyasa jack-of-all-trades, Biffo.

The well-manicured grounds of Sakubva police station were enhanced by a dozen or so colorful but very noisy peacocks that nested there every year, secure in the knowledge that the entire grounds were surrounded by an eight-foot security fence.

One peacock assumed ownership of the station's BSA 650cc Gold Flash motorcycle and, while trying to remove the bird in order to clean the machine, Biffo was attacked and separated from a chunk of his back by the irate peacock.

The Sakubva police station was to obtain an extension to the existing building in the form of a new charge office. Construction was performed by the police pioneers, a section of the force comprising artisans who built and maintained police stations around the country, and a robust English gentleman duly arrived with his gang of builders to build the extension.

Dick and a fellow police officer, a New Zealander aptly nicknamed Kiwi, who was also stationed at Sakubva and had been stationed with David at License Inspectors in Salisbury, struck up a friendship with their English pioneer and shared many conversations over a cup of tea. Their new friend, a woodworker by trade, was forever extoling the virtues of a province in Canada called British Columbia.

"Oh, the countryside, the mountains, the rivers, the climate, the forests; they are all magnificent," and sure enough, as Dick was to find out years later, he was right.

An incident occurred while stationed at Sakubva that is a mystery to this day and concerns the Dangamvura monster. Dangamvura was a small African township some ten miles from the main township of Sakubva and it came about that a bus loaded with passengers had veered off the road late one evening.

When the police arrived at the scene, the driver and all the passengers told the same story. A large monster had appeared on the road ahead, described as being eight or nine feet tall, hairy and full of fury. The driver had swerved to avoid this apparition and consequently crashed.

When investigating further, it appeared that several years previously a local butcher had seized a young boy, chopped him up and sold him as fresh meat to his customers. The butcher had been arrested and convicted, but the locals still believed that the young boy's spirit, in the form of a monster, roamed the Dangamvura township.

The area was patrolled frequently thereafter, seeking perhaps a kudu or eland that might have been mistaken for a large hairy monster, but nothing was found and the monster remains a mystery to this day.

Correspondence between Rhodesia and London had continued throughout the past seven years and it was decided that the time was right for a trip back to Shepherd's Bush. Sean was not yet two and with money being rather tight, it seemed prudent to go before a third seat had to be paid for (children under two did not need a seat and could sit on a parent's lap).

Dick's family had never set eyes on Joyce or Sean and this was put to rights when the three of them took an inexpensive flight to Manchester via Blantyre on a chartered Vickers VC10. Dick's aunt and family had, in the meantime, moved to nearby Liverpool so they would have somewhere to stay upon arrival and could take the train down to London the following day.

Chapter Eight

Flying into Manchester airport, Dick couldn't believe how lush and green everything was. After seven years in Africa, he was used to the dusty brown landscape and the golden savannah and couldn't believe all the rich greenery that he was seeing through the aircraft's window.

They were met by David's uncle and cousin and they drove to Liverpool together. Dick's aunt had stayed at home but gave them a warm welcome, although she was clearly not well, suffering from an as-yet-unknown malady that gave her severe bruises all over her legs, which later turned out to be cancer.

Dick phoned Mom and Dad to tell them that they had arrived safely and the main thing that he will always remember is Mom saying, "You're not David. You don't sound anything like him."

Mentioning this to his cousin when the call was completed, she laughed and remarked, "Well, when you left seven years ago, you spoke with a Cockney accent. Now you speak with a twang, like an Australian."

For the first time, he realized that when speaking with the Africans upon his arrival in Rhodesia, they couldn't understand what he was saying and as time wore on, he began to speak more and more like a Rhodesian so that they could converse. He'd become a Rhodesian and proud of it.

The Rhodesian Birds arrived in Shepherd's Bush the following day. Dick couldn't believe the changes that seemed to have occurred in his absence. As they walked down Bloemfontein Road, it seemed the road was narrower, the houses and the people were smaller and everything was more cramped and crowded, but nothing had really changed. It was just that he had gotten used to Africa's wide-open spaces.

The old house looked bright and cheerful and Dad had done a lot of work to the interior. The landlord, Mr. Everard, was a thing of the past, as Mom and

Dad had bought the house, installed a new bathroom and modernized the house considerably.

Gran and Granddad had passed away and all the bedrooms were now upstairs. Brother John and his wife now had a son and daughter, and, remarkably, their son had been born on the same day and at the same time as Sean.

Joyce caused quite a stir, for she was far from the stereotype British housewife they had perhaps been expecting. Tall, well-spoken and dressed in high heels and a very short mini dress, with immaculate makeup and fancy hairdo she more resembled a model than an African farmer's daughter.

Sean, of course, stole the show and everyone was delighted to see him playing with his cousin Andrew.

A few days later, a great family reunion was organized. Everyone was much older; cousins had grown up and some were married with children of their own. It was a wonderful time.

Dick, Joyce and Sean traveled up to Coventry for a few days to visit Joyce's side of the family. They hadn't seen Joyce since she was a toddler and aunts and uncles all went out of their way to make them welcome.

During the last week of their six-week visit, two unfortunate events occurred: 22-month-old Sean suffered a severe hernia requiring hospitalization and then, just a few days later, Dick's aunt passed away in Liverpool.

An interesting conversation took place one evening between Dick and his mom. She asked him why he hadn't mentioned in any of his letters that he had been the victim of a stabbing some four years previously. He was flabbergasted.

How could she have known about that? It turned out that a couple of years ago, her washing machine had broken down and she went to the local launderette to do her washing. While sitting there, she struck up a conversation with another woman during the course of which they discovered that they each had a son in the BSAP.

The woman said that her son frequently sent her copies of the *Rhodesia Herald*, Salisbury's daily newspaper, and there was an article about a police officer who had been involved in a stabbing incident. She thought his name was Bird.

Of course, they got together again, the newspaper was produced and Dick's attempt at keeping the secret under wraps was a secret no more. It's a small world!

One day, while on a visit up to the City of London, Dick noticed that the old London Bridge, which was built over the river Thames in the 1830s, was being dismantled. After making enquiries, he discovered that the bridge had been purchased by an American, a Mr. Robert McCulloch who intended to number all the stones, transport them to America and reconstruct the bridge somewhere in Arizona.

That's interesting, he thought. *I wonder if he thought he was buying Tower Bridge, for the old London Bridge was no oil painting.*

Dick had to return to duty in Rhodesia, but Sean and his mother remained in London for Sean's operation and the four weeks' recuperation, which incidentally was all performed with the compliments of Britain's National Health Service.

The train journey back to Liverpool and the overnight stay with his uncle and cousin was a sad affair, but Dick caught his charter flight from Manchester back to Salisbury and resumed duty in Umtali on time.

***

The small town of Umtali had a well-supported repertory theater, and when Dick returned, he found that the theater had been scouting the police station for likely participants in a planned presentation of Gilbert and Sullivan's *Pirates of Penzance*. He volunteered and spent the next four weeks rehearsing for the part of both policeman and pirate in the upcoming production.

The cast consisted of about 40 performers—some women, some men, some talented others, not so much. In his role as a pirate, Dick was required to wear boots, some baggy and rather ragged pantaloons, an equally baggy shirt and a headscarf.

For one of the songs, he stood at the front of the stage with a row of scruffy pirates, while behind them stood a row of damsels in distress awaiting rescue. Immediately behind Dick was a young woman, probably in her late teens, who was remarkably attractive and had long, sharp, well-manicured fingernails.

During rehearsals, while standing listening to their producer rambling on about this and that, she noticed a hole in the back of Dick's pantaloons and began probing it with one of her fingers.

Dick constantly asked her to stop, mainly because her mother was standing right next to her, but she persisted. Mere days before Joyce and Sean's return from England, the *Pirates of Penzance* was presented to the people of Umtali to wild applause and complimentary reviews.

The finger was still up to its old tricks, but with guilt and opportunity competing for his attention, he decided that this would be his first and last contribution to the performing arts.

His artistic talents were put to good use, however, not only in helping to paint the backdrops for the operetta, but also with the completion of several oil paintings, some of which were sold and others to adorn the walls of the Bird household.

***

Fully recovered, Sean, now two years of age, became the center of attention and slowly grew into a tall, stocky child who was his parents' pride and joy.

They had made friends with Bobbi and Pete, a young couple living next door to them in Park Vista, and with very little money, they went on a memorable camping holiday with them to Beira in Mozambique. They camped right on the sandy beach, enjoyed cavorting in the clear blue Indian Ocean with Sean and dining in the interestingly different Portuguese restaurants.

Beira was a holiday mecca for Rhodesians. The atmosphere was quite Mediterranean, the culture so different and the people friendly and welcoming. Beira's beaches offered something that landlocked Rhodesians sorely missed and it was a lot closer than Durban.

Dick and his family regularly took the short drive across to Villa de Manica, where a meal for two and a bottle of Mateus Rose could be had for one pound.

Dick's sister Linda, then 21, decided to spend a year in Rhodesia and sailed from Southampton to Cape Town. They drove to Pretoria to meet her on the train from Cape Town and she enjoyed her stay, finding employment in Salisbury and making many friends. She made many short visits to Umtali and was sad to bid farewell to Rhodesia on the journey home.

Before she left, one trip took them to the huge and well-administered Wankie game reserve. The wildlife at Wankie was terrific and having made friends with one of the game rangers and his wife, Dick was given the use of one of their horses. Although it had been some time since Dick had ridden, he managed quite successfully but did not venture far from the camp compound.

The rangers also had their own swimming pool, which David, his wife, Linda, and Sean were given the use of. The only drawback was that each morning before using the pool, they had to scoop out the scorpions that had decided to take a swim the previous night.

On this trip, they also visited the magnificent Victoria Falls, known by the Africans as *Mosi-oa-Tunya,* which translated means The Smoke That Thunders, for even from miles away the roar of the falls can be heard, the ground shakes and the cloud of spray rising above the falls resembles a huge cloud of smoke.

The waterfall is on the Zambezi River, on the border of Zambia and Rhodesia. Although known to local Africans for centuries, it was Scottish missionary David Livingstone who identified the falls in 1855 and named them after Queen Victoria.

The Birds took frequent holidays thanks to the annual six-week leave offered to every member of the force. In late 1972, with his wife several months pregnant with their second child, they set off on a camping trip heading east to reach the Mozambique coast at Nova Sofala and then drove south along the coastal road toward Lourenço Marques.

Their tent was a large old police ridge tent. Quite practical, but it was made of very heavy canvas and sturdy but heavy wooden poles. The whole contraption was transported on the roof rack of their new Renault R12, which allowed plenty of room for bedding, clothing and provisions in the boot.

Their many stops included such delightful towns and villages as Maxixe, Inhambane, Ponta da Barra and Xai Xai. Almost all of their camping spots were on or near the beach and after a daily swim, they would change out of their wet swim wear into comfortable dry clothes, hang the wet costumes on any available tree to dry and set about preparing their evening meal.

One unfortunate aspect of living in Africa is the presence of the maggot fly and it is well known that if forced to hang wet clothing out to dry, it must be well ironed to destroy any larvae that the maggot fly may have deposited. The dry clothing, if not ironed and therefore still containing maggot fly larvae, may pass the larvae onto the wearer's skin, whereupon a tiny maggot will weave its way through the skin and grow.

Thus, Dick incurred an unwelcome visitor into his scrotum and despite valiant efforts by he and his wife to eradicate the problem, it continued to the point where Dick was forced to seek the assistance of a young Portuguese woman at a small pharmacy.

He didn't speak any Portuguese and she didn't speak any English, so sign language was the last resort. Needless to say, after much embarrassment, the proper ointment was acquired and in due course a squirming, wriggling maggot about half an inch long was painfully extracted from the family jewels.

While camping at the beautiful town of Maxixe (pronounced Ma-sheesh), they decided that they should visit Ponta da Barra, an even smaller town on the tip of a peninsula that formed a large bay not far from their camp site. To drive to Ponta da Barra would result in a journey of about 50 miles, but there was an alternative.

A fisherman with a small wooden boat and a dhow-styled sail offered to take them the short distance across the bay, wait for an hour or two and bring them back again. His fee was a pittance, far less than the cost of a gallon of petrol, so they agreed and the three of them drove the short distance down to the shoreline and together with the fisherman climbed upon his rickety old boat and set sail.

The journey took about 20 minutes and was uneventful. The boat tended to leak a bit, but with their captain content to bail with an old tin can, they just relaxed and enjoyed the journey.

Surprisingly, Ponta da Barra had a small post office, so Dick bought a couple of postcards and mailed them to friends back home. They wandered the town, enjoyed the tropical splendor of the setting and then returned to their fisherman for their return journey back to the mainland.

Unlike the trip over, the journey back was a disaster. The boat still leaked, but the wind grew stronger. The tide had fallen considerably and halfway across the bay, the boat came to a grinding halt, resting on a sand bar. The fisherman got out and attempted to push them off, but they were stuck hard and fast.

Their dhow-like sail, made of old, stitched-together flour sacks, was full and attempting to tip the boat over and poor Sean was petrified. Dick and his pregnant wife climbed out to help and the three of them managed to dislodged the boat and continue to the shore—soaking wet.

Dick paid the fisherman and they returned to their car, but to his horror he discovered that he couldn't find his car keys. It then dawned on him that when fishing for some money to mail the postcards, he must have taken his car keys out of his pocket and laid them on the post office counter.

Leaving Sean and his mother standing by their car, he tracked down the fisherman and hired him to return to Ponta da Barra once again. It must be remembered that neither spoke the other's language, which added to the already complicated situation.

However, they did return to Ponta da Barra. Dick gratefully retrieved his car keys from a very pleasant and helpful post office clerk and returned to a relieved, if somewhat scornful, wife.

From Maxixe, they continued down the coast, discovering the wonderful beaches of Xai Xai (pronounced shy-shy). They weren't the only ones to discover Xai Xai for many South Africans, without exception all far better equipped than the Bird family, were busy firing up their small generators, enjoying their well-lit patches of beach, their cold beer and their *braaivleis* (barbecue). It then began to rain—not just normal rain but a torrential downpour.

Having survived the night, they decamped and headed for Komatipoort, which is an entry point into South Africa and once through Komatipoort they headed for Crocodile Bridge and into the southern end of the Kruger National Park. From there, they drove northwards to the park's main camp of Skukuza, where they spent the night in a warm, dry bed.

Kruger National Park offered a perfect opportunity to show Sean an abundance of African wildlife in its natural setting. During their three days at Skukuza, they saw, up close and personal, zebra, giraffe, elephant, kudu, eland, crocodile, Cape buffalo and many other exotic animals as well as fish eagles, owls, herons and hornbills—but alas no lions.

With Christmas Day fast approaching, they departed Kruger National Park via Phalaborwa and headed for Louis Trichardt, where they spent Christmas with Mr. and Mrs. B before heading home to Umtali.

Having served for four years as a section officer, Dick sat his inspector's examination and passed both the written exams and the rigorous depot course. Unfortunately, he had crossed swords with the Assistant Commissioner for that area and consequently was considered too self-opinionated and was told he could wait another year before being promoted.

Being deeply offended by this affront, although it was probably justified, Dick requested a transfer further south to Fort Victoria, sold their house in Umtali and bought a new one in Fort Vic.

Sean was due to start school and as the Birds were expecting a new arrival in the form of son number two, they moved from Umtali to Fort Victoria shortly after their Mozambique adventure. Keith arrived on the scene in April 1973, much to the delight of his elder brother.

While living in Fort Victoria and with their Mozambique camping adventure still fresh in their memory, they bought a small caravan and continued to travel and explore the wonderful sights to be found all around them.

One outstanding feature of Fort Victoria, although it is actually 20 miles out of town, is the famous Zimbabwe Ruins. They are, in fact, the largest collection of ruins in Africa south of the Sahara Desert. Believed to have been built between 1100 and 1400 AD, they extend over 2,000 acres.

The ruins are comprised of huge granite walls constructed with stone blocks to form a series of narrow passageways. There is an acropolis, a great enclosure and a huge phallic symbol some 50 feet high with a base circumference of probably 30 feet or more.

Due to the variety of artifacts that have been discovered at the ruins, coming from as far afield as Persia, China and Arabia, it is presumed that considerable trading took place and that when inhabited, which would have been between the 11th and 15th centuries, the population could have reached as many as 10,000 individuals, most certainly the majority being from the Shona tribe.

Riots and terrorist incursions continued throughout Rhodesia. Sanctions began to bite and petrol became scarce. Thankfully, the Portuguese territory of Mozambique to the east and South Africa to the south both broke UN sanctions and allowed Rhodesia to import and export through their borders. Strict petrol rationing was introduced and many previously imported goods were being manufactured in Rhodesia.

Dick had, by this time, obtained Rhodesian citizenship and thus became a dual citizen of both the United Kingdom and Rhodesia.

Mr. and Mrs. B had, for many years, been annual visitors to England, traveling first class on the Union Castle Line from Cape Town to Southampton and returning every second year with a new Jaguar 3.8, which they collected from the factory in Coventry.

In 1973, Mr. B, always a motoring enthusiast, surpassed himself. Instead of bringing back a Jaguar, he returned home with an Aston Martin DB6, the successor to the DB5 of James Bond fame.

By this time, living in South Africa, what a stir he must have caused as they flashed past the Lion and Elephant hotel on the strip road halfway between Beitbridge and Fort Victoria to visit the Birds.

***

Shortly after Keith was born, Dick retired 'on gratuity' from the BSAP in July 1973 and started a small private security company, Sentinel Security. The company provided uniformed security guards to Fort Victoria's industrial and commercial sector and in two years grew to employ over 50 guards and had a small guard dog section.

The wife of one of Fort Victoria's finest, Yvonne, worked in their small office and was a wonderful administrator, taking care of wages, uniforms and a multitude of tasks. Dick was still required to perform some police duties as part of his national service commitment in addition to seeking new business, overseeing existing contracts and keeping a sharp eye on the bottom line.

Sentinel Security had only one vehicle, a somewhat dilapidated van painted in a style vaguely reminiscent of an old New York police car. Once Dick took some guards to a temporary job about 50 miles from Fort Victoria and on the way home, his van broke down.

Finding himself in something of a pickle, he had no option but to stand on the roadside and thumb a lift. He had only been there for about five minutes when a chauffeur-driven car pulled up and the gentleman in the back seat offered him a lift. During their subsequent conversation, it transpired that he was the general manager of a large sugar, maize and cotton intensive irrigation project in the middle-Sabi area some 200 miles south of Fort Victoria.

By the time Dick was dropped off at home, he had secured a very lucrative contract to provide twelve security guards and a guard dog. It's just wonderful how some things work out: one minute you're stuck out in the middle of nowhere thumbing a lift and the next thing you know you've secured the best contract of the year.

With the business growing and the house mortgage being slowly paid off, Dick was beginning to see a light at the end of the tunnel. His parents flew out for a three-month holiday—their first time overseas and first time flying!

They had a wonderful holiday, spent a week with the in-laws in Louis Trichardt and a week in the Wankie game reserve seeing Africa's wildlife in its natural splendor and, of course, the nearby Victoria Falls.

Dad was in absolute awe at seeing the Africa that he had only dreamed of as a boy. He commented on several occasions that the places he was seeing, even the streets, named after his boyhood heroes Baines, Livingstone and Rhodes, brought back memories of his childhood when living in Bannister's Cottages, Shepherd's Bush so many years ago.

***

Most Rhodesian households had two African servants, one to work in the house and one to work in the garden. Dick and Joyce were no exception, a 'house girl' to do the washing, ironing and housework and a 'garden boy' to cut the lawn, weed and tend to the flower beds and rockeries.

Mom and Dad, especially Mom, wasn't keen on this arrangement at all, but Dad, an avid gardener, seemed to enjoy spending hours with the garden boy pruning rose bushes and cultivating their half-acre of garden. It later turned out that the garden boy in question, a youngster of about eighteen, had spent six months in a Zambian terrorist training camp!

Business took a setback in the summer of 1975. Returning home late one night from a two-week holiday in Durban, Dick found a note written by the lady in his office and pinned to his front door to 'phone middle-Sabi urgently'.

He called the following morning to be told that the development his company was guarding had been attacked by a group of 30 or more terrorists and he should get down there immediately.

Taking his small Alfa Romeo and pathetic .32 pistol, he set off on the 200-mile journey. As he drew close on the dirt road leading up to the compound, he could see soldiers on the road, the newly constructed office buildings full of RPG holes and the smoldering remains of combine harvesters and tractors everywhere.

Things didn't look good. The kindly gentleman who had offered him the security contract barely twelve months ago was fit to be tied. The unarmed guards that were on duty had run for cover, their guard dog had disappeared and had yet to be found, and no one had hit the alarm button, which would have sounded the alert.

With rockets, grenades and automatic gunfire going off everywhere, Dick thought the siren wouldn't have made much difference but decided to keep that opinion to himself.

While trying to placate his client, Dick was interrupted by a soldier carrying a land mine. "Were you the driver of that yellow Alpha Romeo that just came in?" he asked. Dick nodded. "Well, I just dug this up on the dirt road—you missed it by about six inches."

Needless to say, the contract was lost, but the dog was found. No one could really be blamed. It was just another day in Rhodesia!

Dick continued painting and recalls quite clearly working on an oil painting of Sir Francis Chichester's yacht *Gypsy Moth II,* rounding Cape Horn on his epic single-handed voyage around the world. He had his transistor radio on out in the garage where he normally painted, listening to an account of the annual Cape Town to Rio yacht race that was taking place at that time.

Tucked into the back of his mind was the thought that one day he would like to own a sailboat, not necessarily to sail around the world, but to at least experience life at sea with the wind in his sails.

While the Birds were enjoying what they considered to be a pleasant and blissful existence, despite the turmoil of living in a war zone, Mozambique had gained independence from Portugal and had become another source of terrorist training, countenanced by their new African dictator Samora Machel.

The Rhodesian government commenced building what they called a 'cordon sanitaire' along the Mozambique border. It was basically a minefield, but progress was constantly interrupted by terrorists who would come in at night and sabotage the bulldozers and excavators used to clear and flatten the terrain. Consequently, part of the police's anti-terrorist duties was to protect the equipment and operators.

Dick and his fellow 'volunteers' were dispatched to the border for this purpose. Two weeks in the Zambezi valley, wearing camouflage gear and weighed down with backpack, semi-automatic FNs and plenty of ammunition was a good weight loss program.

Dick can clearly recall his flight to the border area in a vintage Rhodesian Air Force Dakota DC4. The flight didn't take very long and their landing was not on an airstrip but in a field. During the flight, he didn't see any sign of sky; only trees flashing past the windows as if in a train.

It was later explained that the aircraft was deliberately flown down a long river valley, keeping as low an altitude as possible to avoid surface-to-air missiles whose heat-seeking device didn't kick in until it reached a certain height well above that of their aircraft.

His 'stick' of five police reservists took turns standing guard over the machinery and equipment. In the dead of night and totally alone in a bleak and hostile setting, it was quite an eerie experience. Obviously, silence and concealment were imperative, and even one hour seemed like ten.

The 'stick' rotated station every two hours, so everyone had the opportunity to sleep, but it was not ideal with only the bare ground for a mattress and the thought of being awakened at any moment by the sound of explosions and machine gun fire.

After two weeks in the bush with no opportunity to wash, shave or change clothes, it was a relief to get home. However, his welcome was rather an anti-climax, being that he stank worse than a pig and looked even worse.

***

On the sporting scene, while living in Fort Victoria, Dick met up with an Irishman who managed the local brewery and they played tennis together for several years. Although Dick was a lousy tennis player, the Irishman wasn't much better and they kept at it, enjoying a few beers together after the game.

In 1976, Dick decided that the writing was on the wall when it came to Rhodesia's future. Rhodesia, having made a wonderful stand against impossible odds, was going the way of the rest of Africa, with either ZAPU's Joshua Nkomo or ZANU's Robert Mugabe destined to become the new dictator of a one-party state.

With this future in mind and, as so many had predicted, the country was, in fact, rapidly heading toward destruction, productive farmland was to be turned into goat pastures and the economy would go downhill fast. Well done, Harold Wilson.

Dick determined that it was time to leave not only Rhodesia, but also the continent of Africa. However, with limited resources, he decided that the best step toward moving overseas was to emigrate to South Africa and use that as a steppingstone to finding a new home elsewhere.

His last duty in the police reserve was to draw an FN rifle from the armory and to drive a clapped-out Land Rover 20 miles to the top of a *kopje* (small hill) close to the Zimbabwe Ruins. Once there, he had to set up radio communications with someone at a similar location close to Beitbridge.

As there had been so many terrorist ambushes on the 300-mile stretch of road between Fort Victoria and Beitbridge, a convoy was arranged twice a day for civilian vehicles. Military vehicles with mounted machine guns traveled at the front and rear of the convoy and radio communications were maintained between Dick and the convoy until the halfway point when Beitbridge would take over.

No attacks were made on the convoy during Dick's tours of duty, but on one occasion, while sitting alone at the top of the kopje, he heard several bursts of automatic gunfire below.

He discovered over his radio that there was contact with a group of armed terrorists at the foot of the kopje and considering his options—one rifle and about a dozen rounds of ammunition—he chose to climb the nearest tree and wait things out.

As things turned out, the matter was taken care of down below and he returned home safely.

One of the last things that the Bird family did before leaving Rhodesia was take a drive out to take a last look at the Zimbabwe Ruins. They found the ruins to be deserted, for the bush war had destroyed tourism and the majority of locals felt it was safer to stay in town than to venture out into the bush.

Baboons had virtually taken over the ruins and were running rampant over the huge granite walls that had once been so magnificent. It was with a heavy heart that, in late 1976, with their dog Scamp and their small caravan in tow, the Birds drove south across Beit Bridge for the last time and made their way into South Africa.

Departing from the Rhodesian side, Dick recalls the immigration officer's final words: "another family on the chicken run."

Understandably, Rhodesia did not want the dwindling European population to leave and therefore instituted exchange control measures, which meant taking no money and no motor vehicles out of the country. Having sold their house and business, they had a considerable amount of money that had to remain in Rhodesia, earning little or no interest.

The government later introduced a measure whereby the funds could be sent out of the country after several years had lapsed, whereupon it would be remitted over a seven-year period.

Emigrants were permitted, however, to take possessions, including furniture and caravans and fortunately Dick had opened a savings account in South Africa several years earlier and had access to limited South African Rands. Part of these funds were used to buy a small pick-up truck in South Africa, drive it up to Fort Victoria, hook up the caravan and depart.

Arrangements were made to ship the furniture to Johannesburg and place it in storage. Equally luckily, Dick had been able to purchase four return tickets on the Union Castle shipping line from Cape Town to Southampton, at a date to be determined, before leaving Salisbury.

In later life, Dick was to realize that the Rhodesia that existed upon his arrival and during his early years there was the best, the happiest and the most prosperous country that he had ever had the good fortune to live in.

Chapter Nine

In early 1976, they arrived in South Africa and headed directly for Johannesburg, where they parked their tiny caravan in a convenient caravan park and Dick set about finding a job. Sean was quickly enrolled in a local school, smartly decked out in his school uniform and all four of them and their dog Scamp were to live in that caravan for almost six months!

Within a week, Dick was hired as head of security for a large factory in Langlaagte that specialized in manufacturing lighting fixtures and their various components. The factory and office complex were opposite a huge and ugly mine dump similar to those seen over several parts of Johannesburg, which were created by the huge mines in the never-ending quest for gold.

In later years, when better technology was developed, some of these mine dumps were actually re-mined to extract gold that had been missed in earlier years.

The owners of Consolidated Lighting were very concerned with the terrorist threat and unrest that would soon arrive on their doorstep and were anxious to take the necessary precautions.

Having been through the situation that was now facing South Africa, Dick was in a perfect situation to organize security staffing and training to set out plans for dealing with bomb threats, and prepare the 300 or so employees for civil disturbances and any emergencies that might arise.

After six months of living in the caravan, the Birds rented a house in the suburb of Mondeor and after just over one year with Consolidated Lighting, David took a leave of absence and, using the Union Castle Line tickets purchased in Rhodesia, the Bird family, sans dog, took the train from Johannesburg to Cape Town.

They were fascinated upon reaching Cape Province to see mile upon mile of pristine vineyards. They were witnessing the famous vineyards of

Stellenbosch and Dick made a promise to visit the Cape again one day and sample the products of those magnificent vineyards.

Upon arrival in Cape Town, they headed directly to the docks where they boarded the Union Castle Ocean liner, the *Windsor Castle*, which would head up the west coast of Africa to the Spanish Canary Islands before traveling through the Bay of Biscay and arriving in Southampton.

Due to the current oil crisis at that time and in an effort to conserve fuel, the voyage was slower than usual, taking almost two weeks. It was also Queen Elizabeth II's Silver Jubilee and the Union Castle line provided spectacular entertainment along the way. Their two-night stopover at Las Palmas was a treat in itself and gave them the opportunity to tour the main island of Gran Canaria and take in the sights.

For Dick, the most fascinating was the volcano. Standing on the edge and looking down into the huge core of the volcano, he was amazed to see a small farm, complete with farmhouse, with well laid out and fertile fields and a vehicle. How to get down there and back up again was a mystery, for he could see no road, track or pathway.

Upon leaving Las Palmas, their ship crossed the Bay of Biscay. Numerous flying fish dived, flew and wallowed before the bow of the ship and he learned that the bay is prolific in its multitude of fish, including barracudas, angelfish, sharks and bonefish. This was Dick's first time seeing flying fish. Seeing them in such huge numbers and realizing that they actually do fly was quite an experience.

Once through the bay, it was exciting to enter the English Channel and begin searching for The Needles, a row of three stacks of chalk that rose about 100 feet out of the sea off the western extremity of the Isle of Wight with The Needles Lighthouse at the western end of the formation. Once sighted, it was only a short time before their ship entered the Solent and docked at Southampton.

Upon arrival at Southampton, they were met with a nasty surprise when it was announced that the stevedores at the Southampton docks were on strike. A request was made for all able-bodied men to unload the vessel of all the passengers' luggage, whereupon they could disembark.

Dick, of course, volunteered along with several dozen passengers and all the various suitcases and trunks, suitably labeled, were eventually deposited ashore in strict alphabetical order. While passengers traipsed back and forth from ship to shore carrying mountains of luggage, several striking stevedores slouched in doorways and corridors, casting sarcastic and offensive remarks about scabs and sellouts, which were sensibly ignored.

Mom, Dad and Linda were at the dockside watching all this unfold but were powerless to help. Eventually, the passengers were permitted to clear customs and immigration and Dick and family began their four weeks ashore.

This was the family's second trip to England since Dick left in 1962. Dick's parents had sold their house in London and bought a fairly new one in the small town of Bedhampton in Hampshire.

It was now 1977! They took the opportunity of Mom and Dad's offer to take care of the children and had a week in Cannes on the French Riviera and a short visit to Guernsey in the Channel Islands, where Mr. and Mrs. B were on holiday.

Due to limited finances, their week in Cannes was spent on a fairly tight budget. Their hotel was in town, a couple of miles from the famous beach and marina, but they enjoyed the walks and watching the rich and famous at play. This was their first visit to France and Dick was determined to see as much of the French Riviera as possible. The beaches of Cannes were busy, the girls topless, the weather beautiful and the city clean.

Everything was so different from anything Dick had experienced before that he vowed to see so much more of this wonderful world. He was determined that he would never allow their two children to confine their activities but rather encourage them to broaden their knowledge and experiences by showing them as much of the world as he could.

One day, it was decided to take a bus along the Cote d'Azur as far as Saint Tropez. An early start was necessary, so they boarded an empty bus at 6.00 am. The bus would take them as far as St. Raphael, where they would change buses to St. Tropez.

Their driver, a man in his early twenties, drove sedately along the beautiful route; the morning weather was magnificent and the views absolutely stunning. After traveling approximately 10 miles, they caught sight of another passenger waiting to be picked up at the roadside, a very pretty young woman dressed in a crisp blue-and-white polka dot dress with a belted waist.

The driver stopped and she hopped aboard. She seemed to know their driver and as they drove away, she stood beside him chatting and then sat on his lap. The Birds, the driver's only passengers, gave each other knowing looks and watched from their bench seat halfway down the bus.

Sure enough, after traveling about another ten miles, the bus pulled over beside a large hedge. The driver switched off the engine and, without a word to his two passengers, led the young lady off the bus and behind the hedge.

Fifteen minutes later they reappeared, brushing bits of grass off their clothing. The driver started his engine. She resumed her seat on his lap and they arrived at the St. Raphael bus station in time to catch their bus to St. Tropez. Dick never did see her pay her bus fare! Viva la France!

Dick found Saint Tropez to be a larger town than expected, but was disappointed that he didn't get a chance to meet up with Bridget Bardot, its most famous resident.

They did find several restaurants that were on the sandy beach and Dick well recalls watching one young woman seated at one of the tables, topless, trying to eat her meal and having to keep pushing her large breasts aside to get to it!

The bus ride back to Cannes was less interesting, although the small seaside town of Saint Raphael, with its small beachside hotels and beautiful beaches, really caught Dick's eye and was placed on his bucket list for future reference.

***

Wherever Dick lived, be it in England, Rhodesia or South Africa, holidays and travel were always on his mind. In England, it was limited to camping trips with the scouts, his 800-mile cycling cum camping adventure in south and west England and a one-week hitch-hiking holiday in the Netherlands.

Touring Rhodesia and South Africa, first in tents and later in his tiny twelve-foot caravan which offered better prospects and the Birds made many trips throughout the area visiting game reserves, the Garden Route, the magnificent wine lands of Stellenbosch, Table Mountain and the beautiful city of Cape Town.

One Christmas, they took the caravan to Coffee Bay on the wild coast of the Transkei, where they met up with Joyce's old flat-mate Jean, her husband John and their three children who were camping in tents. At that time, the

Transkei, although part of South Africa, operated as a nominally independent democracy but remained internationally unrecognized.

Coffee Bay was a tiny speck on the map that could only be reached by traveling along 80 miles of a corrugated dirt road and was well over 1,000 miles south of Johannesburg.

Many hours were spent enjoying the beaches of Coffee Bay. Dick had a small battery-operated tape recorder, which they used continually to provide music. On one memorable occasion, a group of three young African girls singing Christmas carols approached them on the beach.

While they were singing, Dick switched the recorder on and when they had finished and received their *bon sella* (gift), he replayed their singing to them. Their reaction was unforgettable. They had obviously never seen or heard of a tape recorder before. It was pure magic and a treat that Dick would always remember fondly.

A local native showed off his fishing skills by diving stark naked into the Indian Ocean to search for saltwater spiny lobster, better known in South Africa as crayfish, which he sold for 50 cents each. It was noted that their fisherman had lost a couple of fingers in the course of this dangerous occupation, but despite wearing no clothes, his family jewels seemed to be in fine fettle.

The two dozen crayfish, which they bought from him, comprised their Christmas dinner, supplemented with various salads and vegetables and with the table decorated with a myriad of wild flame lilies, Rhodesia's national flower. In Dick's opinion, it was the best Christmas dinner he'd ever had.

Following Christmas, the weather changed from glorious blue skies to torrential thunderstorms. Their friends' tents were soon drenched and all nine of them crammed into the twelve-foot caravan to ride out the storm.

The following morning, Dick and John decided to walk back along Coffee Bay's only access road, across the low-level bridge that was only about a foot above the rising water level, and assess the road conditions.

After a mile or so, they decided that the road was in sufficiently good shape to get John's family back to Johannesburg and that they would break camp and return home. Dick's decision was to remain behind until after the New Year.

Returning to the camp site, they were horrified to see that in the short time they had been away, storm water from the surrounding mountains had completely covered the bridge by a flash flood. What had been a gentle, trickling brook had become a raging torrent over 100 feet wide that was washing trees, debris and drowned or drowning cattle down to the ocean.

Furthermore, it was well known that sharks patrolled the mouths of such rivers when in full flood, where easy meals were in abundance.

What to do? They had no way of crossing the river; it would have been suicide to try swimming, and they had no way of contacting their families on the other side.

While gazing at the raging waters, a man and woman appeared on the opposite bank with a canoe. Watching in disbelief, they saw them launch their canoe into the raging torrent. Paddling desperately upstream, they made steady, though somewhat wobbly, progress to the other shore.

When they grabbed their canoe to help them ashore, they learned that the couple was so anxious to reach their family that they had stolen the canoe in desperation. It didn't take long for Dick and John to rectify their situation— they would board the canoe and return it to its rightful owners. What a ride from hell that turned out to be!

Once back at camp, their friends dismantled their sodden tents and decided to cross the low-level bridge as soon as the water receded sufficiently. This took several hours, but eventually, when the bridge was only about twelve inches below water level, the Bird family watched with trepidation as their friends' Peugeot station wagon forded the river and the bridge to gain access to the far bank.

Dick and family, their caravan now restored to normal, resumed their holiday. The sun shone out of a blue sky and the question was how to spend the remainder of their holiday at Coffee Bay.

Dick, some years previously, had begun accompanying himself on the guitar and with enough beverages inside him and a reasonable repertoire of songs, he considered himself sufficiently adept to perform in public.

There was a small hotel in Coffee Bay with a small bar and Dick and Joyce spent a memorable evening there with David performing with his guitar. The bar was crowded and obviously most of the patrons had had too much to drink for his music and singing went down well and too much acclaim.

The following evening was New Year's Eve and Coffee Bay's small hotel was planning a New Year's Eve party, which Dick decided they would attend. As Sean and Keith were used to sleeping in the car when Mom and Dad went out for the evening, they were bedded down and fast asleep just outside the hotel and were checked upon periodically.

The party was attended by several dozen holiday makers and they were invited to join a family group sitting at a nearby table. When told of the storm damage that sent half their group packing, the family said that they had a small holiday cottage nearby and insisted that they spend New Year's Day with them.

The following day was exceptional. Their hosts were so hospitable, friendly and very interesting. Their cottage was perched on top of a small rise with magnificent views and Dick was fascinated by the history surrounding the area. Coffee Bay was named in 1893, after a shipwreck lost its cargo of coffee beans in the bay and turned the waters brown.

What was even more astonishing was the history surrounding a small peninsula that jutted out into the ocean, known as Grosvenor Point. The name dates back to the days of the East Indiamen sailing ships that plied the oceans between England and India.

In 1782, an East Indiaman named the *Grosvenor* was shipwrecked on the point. All passengers and crew were safely hauled ashore, but the ship broke up and all its rumored treasure was lost.

Many books have since been written about the *Grosvenor,* but the earliest and most famous is titled *The Wreck of the Grosvenor* by William Clark Russell, first published in 1877.

For over 200 years, fortune hunters have searched for the fabulous treasures that were reputed to have been on the ill-fated ship, but despite several bizarre schemes that have been launched, little has been found.

Legends of how the survivors were captured by local natives, the men slaughtered and the women and children taken as slaves abound. Three men actually escaped and walked several hundred miles south to the settlement of East London, where they told of the disaster.

It is said that some of the present-day native population still retain the aquiline noses and European features bred into them by the female passengers of the *Grosvenor*. Stranger than fiction? Look it up!

Chapter Ten

Once back in Johannesburg, Dick took another plunge into the unknown. He renegotiated his full-time job with Consolidated Lighting into a part-time position and started a new security company, this time preparing emergency planning programs and staff training for industrial and commercial operations that were too small to warrant a full-time security staff.

The company, Security Advisory Services, operated out of a small office shared with another security-related business and slowly began to produce results with one client pressuring Dick to provide a security guard service similar to the one in Rhodesia.

While Dick was considering this, he received an unexpected phone call from an old acquaintance, a Greek businessman named Nick, whom David knew as the owner of a drive-in cinema and a dry-cleaning service in Fort Victoria.

Aware of Dick's past police experience and that he had owned a private security company in Fort Victoria, he said that he was in Durban looking into the purchase of a large security company and asked if Dick would be interested in moving down there to help him manage it.

Durban was a prime holiday destination in South Africa and a huge improvement over Johannesburg, so Dick was keen to hear more and flew down to Durban to meet him.

Durban, the third most populous city in South Africa, is situated on the Indian Ocean and is ethnically diverse, with large Zulu, White and Indian/Asian populations.

The security company that his friend was considering buying was well established and lucrative but very, very expensive and would involve a large bank loan. Dick proposed an alternative. How about starting a new security company from scratch that would offer not only security guards but cash-in-transit services, wage packaging, alarm installation and monitoring and, of course, dogs?

He stressed that the cash outlay would be a fraction of the cost of this established company and would not require incurring any debt, but Dick insisted on owning 50 percent of the company with no capital investment and a salary from day one.

After some debate, Dick's proposal was adopted. He discontinued Security Advisory Services, resigned from Consolidated Lighting, packed up their belongings and moved the family to Durban, where he and his friend established their new company, Guardforce.

The Durban move turned out to be an excellent decision. The climate was incredible, the white population all English-speaking (as opposed to Afrikaans) and the business opportunities plentiful.

Now living in a rented house, and the tiny caravan having gone the way of the dodo, their fledgling security company became a well-known provider of a variety of security services and Nick went on to do what he always did best, to buy small or struggling businesses, reorganize them to become efficient and profitable, and resell them at considerable profit.

Once Guardforce was established, Dick was able to purchase a lovely house with a swimming pool, high on a hill overlooking the Indian Ocean in the suburb of Glenashley. He eventually succeeded in purchasing his partner's 50 percent of the business and in a relatively short space of time developed it into a highly profitable undertaking.

It was around this time that Mr. and Mrs. B decided to sell their house in Louis Trichardt and move to Durban, where they purchased a beautiful apartment in Glenashley's only high-rise complex, high on a hill overlooking the ocean.

Once again, Dick began playing bad tennis, this time at the tennis courts in the nearby suburb of La Lucia. He met up with a fellow Englishman who owned a printing business in Durban and they played doubles or singles every Saturday morning followed this time, not by a few beers as he had with his Irish tennis partner in Fort Victoria but with orange juice.

The Birds became good friends with David's tennis partner Don and his wife and frequently entertained at each other's houses.

Sadly, the family dog Scamp, now in his tenth or eleventh year, was attacked by a much larger dog and was so badly injured that he had to be put down.

They had also made some new friends who lived nearby, Chris and Lorraine. Chris had been born in Canada and his father lived in British Columbia.

The two couples met frequently until, in late 1980, Chris and Lorraine emigrated from South Africa to Canada, where they settled in the small town of Penticton in the Okanagan Valley, British Columbia.

Does this ring a bell? Remember the police pioneer who rambled on about its countryside, mountains, rivers and so on?

Both Sean and Keith had schools within cycling distance of the new house and the Birds were expecting a third child. Bearing in mind Dick's intention to leave the African continent, it was decided that after their baby was born, they should visit Chris and Lorraine in Canada and check out the lie of the land.

Guardforce went from strength to strength but became such a stressful business to operate that in 1981 Dick sold the security guard side of the business to an old Rhodesian acquaintance. The security guard business was fraught with problems, primarily one of staffing.

Night after night, David was out checking to make sure his employees were vigilant in keeping watch, only to find them sleeping, sometimes with their guard dogs sleeping at their feet. He purchased all kinds of devices to encourage them to greater effort—devices such as night watchmen's clocks that required keys located at strategic points throughout the complex to be inserted at fifteen-minute intervals into a clock which could be inspected the following morning.

One particular guard, a loyal older man with a delightful nature, had been constantly reprimanded for not clocking in properly. He was given one final warning and took the warning to heart. When checking the clock, the following morning, David was relieved to see that it was being used properly.

He had no sooner relaxed when the telephone rang, with the client complaining that the premises had been broken into the previous night and that a typewriter had been stolen from the office. The guard was consequently dragged out of bed to explain.

"But boss," he complained. "You told me that if I didn't put the correct key in the clock every fifteen minutes, I would be fired. I did see a man climbing the fence, but I had only a minute or two to get over to the far side of the premises to key my clock and when I returned, the man had disappeared. I didn't notice the broken window!"

Go figure.

Some security guards stole from the premises they were supposed to be guarding; others just deserted their posts or had a girlfriend cuddle up with them for company.

These incidents of incompetence, laziness and outright dereliction of duty were not limited to African security guards. Guardforce maintained a 24-hour control room that housed a state-of-the-art alarm monitoring system manned by a white security officer.

This individual had three responsibilities: first, to acknowledge and act upon any alarms raised on the monitor; second, to attend to any radio messages coming over the air from guards equipped with walkie-talkie radios; and third, to answer the telephone.

An alarm contract had recently been secured with a chain of betting shops. The general manager was particularly concerned with armed hold-ups during their daytime operations and panic buttons had been installed for employees to activate if necessary. The panic button would send a signal to the Guardforce control room, which in turn would contact the nearest police station.

Sure enough, a hold-up occurred. The employee pressed the panic button and handed over the cash. The security officer pressed the acknowledge button on the monitor but failed to read the code nine (hold-up in progress) on the print-out and did not react appropriately; in fact, he didn't react at all.

When the client phoned Dick, he explained that although his employee claimed to have pressed the panic button, he suspected that she didn't due to the frightening situation that she was in. When Dick checked the print-out on the monitor, he discovered that the panic code had indeed been received and acknowledged.

He admonished the security officer, fired him on the spot, and went to see the client. The client was amazed when David told him that the employee was in no way to blame. She had acted admirably in hitting the panic button and that it was entirely the fault of Guardforce that no immediate action had been taken.

Then came the biggest surprise of all. Instead of his client blowing a fuse, canceling the contract and threatening to sue, he said that he appreciated Dick's honesty in admitting his company's failure and would consider the matter closed.

The contract would remain in force. This cemented Dick's lifelong belief that honesty is the best policy and he has stuck with this attitude his whole life, even though it has sometimes been to his distinct disadvantage.

While living in Durban, his life was pretty good. The large Indian population added a new dimension to the South African way of life and Dick found that many of the Indians he encountered were well educated, intelligent and very easy to get along with.

Indian restaurants abounded, but one restaurant with the rather colonial name of the British Middle East Sporting and Dining Club was his absolute favorite. The building was old with creaking wooden floorboards, but the curries the restaurant produced were unbelievable.

Waiters, clad all in white and wearing red fezzes and in bare feet added to the charm and atmosphere and although Dick will be the first to admit that, although as a general rule he doesn't really like food, this restaurant fare was an exception.

Not only were the curries good, but a waiter came around with a trolley containing a huge assortment of sambals such as chopped nuts, sliced banana, chopped tomatoes and onions to name just a few, to sprinkle on top.

***

Having disposed of the guard business, his new company provided only cash-in-transit, wage packaging and intruder alarms. It continued to be profitable, but he still felt the need to move on. South Africa was facing mounting pressure to abandon its apartheid policy and hand over control of the country to majority rule and after seeing how badly that had worked out in Zimbabwe he was determined to leave.

With this in mind, the Birds, all five of them including four-month-old Karen, flew to England for a week and then on to British Columbia's Okanagan Valley, where they stayed with their old friends from Durban, Chris and Lorraine.

They rented a small motorhome and toured British Columbia and northern Washington state, looking for somewhere or something that would appeal to them both. They eventually decided that they would develop and open a cottage winery in the Okanagan Valley, which would be named Ronayne after Dick's mother's family.

Small wineries in the Okanagan Valley, referred to as cottage wineries, had sprung up in the region and were proving surprisingly successful, especially with the production of white wines whose grapes adapted well to the arid semi-desert terrain and hot summers that were a feature of the area.

In summer, the temperature would reach over 100 degrees, yet in winter, it would drop well below freezing.

One of the British Columbia government's requirements was that in order to grant a permit for a cottage winery, the vineyard had to contain at least ten acres of grape vines. Additional grapes could thereafter be purchased from local vineyards to boost wine production and wines could then be produced on-site.

The idea seemed perfect to Dick, who had no clue regarding his own limits and capabilities. They could build a house and winery on the property and provide a tourist destination right on the Trans-Canada Highway. The more cottage wineries created, the more of a tourist attraction the area would become and Dick envisaged a smaller scale of something eventually developing along the lines of Stellenbosch in South Africa or Napa Valley in northern California.

He enlisted a local real estate agent to search for a suitable location and then returned to Durban to apply to the Canadian consulate in South Africa for immigration to Canada. During the interview, he explained that he was purchasing land in the Okanagan Valley, where he proposed establishing a cottage winery.

The official conducting the interview asked if the winery would be creating job opportunities for Canadians and David assured him that it would. He was then told that if the background checks were satisfactory, he would receive immigration documents in due course.

Upon returning to Durban, he negotiated the sale of his cash-in-transit, wage packaging and security alarm business to the same person who had previously purchased the security guard company. He then began taking courses on wine, viticulture and wine-making with the Stellenbosch Farmers' Winery.

Their house in Glenashley was sold to a couple who agreed to take over the ownership of their beautiful golden Labrador named Tiger, and they moved into a rented waterfront apartment, where they waited for six months for their Canadian immigration papers to arrive.

Their wait for Canadian immigration documents was a long one, but the boys continued to attend school and David, Joyce and two-year-old Karen enjoyed living close to the beach and downtown Durban. Eventually, their immigrant papers arrived and they booked flights to Penticton in the Okanagan Valley via England and Calgary.

Chapter Eleven

After spending a few days in England visiting Mom, Dad and the rest of the family, they flew onwards to British Columbia landing at Penticton airport via Calgary in the late afternoon of 31 October, where their friends Chris and Lorraine were to meet them.

Strangely, all three of their children were in weird fancy dress and face paint. It wasn't until later that they discovered that October 31st, All Hallows Eve, was celebrated as Halloween in North America.

Unlike London, where All Hallows Eve was to Dick's recollection a somewhat somber and insignificant occasion, and in southern Africa, where it wasn't celebrated at all, in Canada and the United States, all the children apparently donned fancy dress and went begging for sweets.

This was only one of many differences that Dick had noted between England, Southern Africa and North America.

"Why," people kept asking him, "do you call yourself Dick? Even your wife calls you Dicky. Is your name Richard?"

He explained over and over again that Dick or Dicky was a common nickname for anyone with the surname Bird, but they didn't understand. He eventually discovered that people in North America didn't refer to birds as dicky birds, even to young children, so he decided that he would revert to his proper Christian name and from that point on, with the exception of his wife and many friends in Zimbabwe and South Africa, he once again became known as David.

The following weeks were a blur. David first went to visit the 35 acres of land, which he had foolishly bought sight unseen. The land bordered Canada's Highway 1, which at that time was Canada's main cross-country highway and therefore in an excellent location.

The land was situated in the small town of Keremeos, the name originating from the native Indian word *keremeyeus* meaning 'creek which cuts its way through the flats' and refers to Keremeos Creek, which flows down from the Upper Benchlands to the Similkameen River. The town lies south of Penticton and some 300 miles east of Vancouver and the Pacific coast.

The land comprised about 10 acres of woodland, which was flat and suitable for a vineyard. The remainder was the stony base of a huge mountain known locally as Pudding Head, with a level bench about ten feet higher than the forest of large pines.

The trees would have to be removed to make room for the vineyard. The stone and gravel bench was large enough to accommodate their house, the winery and five or six small cottages for vacation rentals.

They rented an unfurnished, wood-framed house in the small town and close to their 35 acres. With their imported furniture and household effects stored in Vancouver, they furnished the house with bits and pieces borrowed from Chris and Lorraine and from Chris' family, who lived close by.

David contracted with a local heavy machinery company to supply a D8 bulldozer and operator to push over and uproot the many large trees and level the ground in preparation for planting.

It was now late November and winter had set in with a vengeance. Canada's snow and freezing weather had replaced the beginning of a hot and humid Durban summer and reality began to dawn on them. Cold winter gear was purchased along with two vehicles, a half-ton Chevrolet pick-up truck with snow tires and chains and a small Honda Civic hatchback.

Two local men with trucks and chain saws agreed to help strip, cut up and remove the trees with David, who struggled to operate a newly purchased 24-inch Husqvarna chain saw. The two men agreed to accept the newly logged timber in payment for their labor, and over a period of three or four weeks the trees were either removed or burned, ten acres were leveled and the project was on schedule.

A local winery generously offered considerable help in getting Ronayne Winery started and even went so far as to offer the use of their equipment to crush and ferment the Ronayne grapes until David could have his winery properly equipped.

Although it would take some years before the newly planted vines could be expected to produce acceptable grapes, once the vineyard was planted, the winery would be allowed to purchase grapes from local growers and commence producing wine under the Ronayne label.

The next step was to purchase and plant suitable rootstock and install appropriate trellises and a drip feed irrigation system. Then would come the task of building a house and a warehouse to accommodate the wine press, bottling plant and wine-making equipment. It was also necessary to obtain an easement to gain legal access to the property from Highway 1 and herein lay a problem.

A government survey team advised that Pudding Head, the mountain behind the property, was considered a landslide hazard and that no easement, buildings or public access would be permitted without a huge berm first being constructed as a catchment for any rocks or boulders that may cascade down the mountainside.

David began to realize that the expense of this, in fact the entire enterprise, was beyond his ability to finance and resorted to requesting a provincial government loan to assist with the financing of his winery. This was duly submitted, considered and rejected, which left him with no option but to come up with a plan B.

After spending six months in Keremeos and spending a great deal of time and money, David hastily conceived Plan B, which consisted of abandoning the whole idea of a cottage winery and instead moving to Vancouver and starting a Canadian version of Guardforce. It should be noted that the Okanagan Valley has since developed into a thriving grape-growing and wine-making area with many cottage wineries now in existence. He was just a little ahead of his time.

Before leaving Keremeos, he learned that Queen Elizabeth II, who was on a tour of Canada, was to visit the small town of Vernon some 80 miles to the north. Unwilling to miss the opportunity of seeing her again, he drove up to Vernon and stood among a small crowd of perhaps 200 people to listen to Her Majesty give a brief but heart-warming speech.

He was interested in learning that when she attended a luncheon in her honor, apparently a local wine from the Okanagan Valley was served.

Sadly, departing the town of Keremeos, David duly moved to the affluent suburb of West Vancouver, rented a small house in this very desirable area from a Chinese gentleman and retrieved their furniture from storage. David met with the local bank manager, opened an account and prepared to unleash Guardforce onto the Vancouver scene.

An anecdote connected with David's bank, and in fact with a North American custom frequently encountered, is worth relating. Every time David went to visit the teller, the busty blonde women would greet him with the same "Good day. How are you?"

The first time this happened, David thought how different this was from the friendly but business-like 'hello' he was used to receiving when banking in Rhodesia or South Africa. He'd never been asked how he was. It happened time and time again until David thought that if the woman was asking him a question, she was entitled to an answer.

The next time he visited the teller, he put it to the test.

"Good day. How are you?" she asked.

There were other customers waiting in line behind him, but he nonetheless replied, telling her that he was feeling a bit under the weather, thought he had a cold coming on and was not enjoying the thought of another winter which would soon be on its way.

The blonde lady gave him a strange look, then laughed and asked, "Why are you telling me all this?"

Go figure! It was just the North American way of being polite, like saying hello, but not a question at all and not at all sincere.

Once established in their rented house and with their furniture and personal effects recovered from storage, David set about the task of getting the business started, securing some contracts and hiring suitable personnel.

Within a relatively short period of time, a contract was entered into with the Vancouver transit authority to provide night watchmen, one at each of their six bus depots. Suitable personnel were hired and trained, and Guardforce was launched.

After a small Renault vehicle was purchased and adorned with the Guardforce livery and spotlight, David began his nocturnal visits to the sites in question, checking on personnel and slowly introducing them to his security philosophy, which was basically to be viewed as a deterrent, not as a confrontational presence, except as a last resort.

Private security, in David's opinion, should be used not to effect an arrest but to deter those with criminal intent from selecting the premises being guarded. If they were committed to criminal activity, they could do it somewhere else!

A second contract soon followed, which required a night watchman every night, dawn to dusk, at a Vancouver shopping center. Two more suitable men were employed and working separate shifts they became a dependable and reliable team.

Just when things were beginning to take shape, the Vancouver transit authority decided not to renew their contract, probably due to a lower bid from a competing company, and Guardforce was left with only one contract, two employees, no immediate prospects and with David's funds fast drying up. What to do now?

Recalling the conversation with the Canadian immigration official back in South Africa, David was under the mistaken impression that his Canadian resident permit was conditional upon establishing a business that would provide employment opportunities for Canadians.

Therefore, he believed that seeking employment himself was not an option and therefore began searching for a business that he could purchase.

He eventually settled on buying a small sporting goods store in the suburb of Burnaby, already named D and J Sporting Goods. The initials fit as his wife's name began with a 'J' and it seemed just meant to be.

The store had a regular clientele and specialized in the sports of ice hockey and lacrosse, two sports that David knew absolutely nothing about. It had one full-time employee and three part-time employees who were in high school but were very knowledgeable about hockey and lacrosse.

Things went well for a while, but sales slowly began to drop off as more and more of the store's clientele became aware that the new owner knew little or nothing about their sports. To offset this problem, David expanded the range of equipment carried in the store to include running, tennis, basketball, soccer and a broader range of apparel but with little success.

During the quiet times, of which there were plenty, David had lots of time to chat with his sole full-time employee Kevin, who was nineteen at the time, reminiscing about Africa and recollecting the wonderful experiences that he had in the 20 years that he had lived there.

Not realizing the seeds of discontent that he was planting but slowly impressing upon the lad the opportunities for travel, excitement and adventure that were just there waiting for a nineteen-year-old to seize, David had, in fact, been giving him the Miss Dexter treatment!

Kevin, probably seeing where D & J Sporting Goods was headed before David did, eventually seized the challenge and booked a flight to Durban.

David provided him with a good contact in Durban who helped to introduce him into the local culture and set him on the road to travel, adventure and success. A replacement was now needed and although one was found easily enough, David could clearly see that things were going from bad to worse.

***

The Bird family still managed to take holidays from time to time, all of them successful camping trips. They enjoyed traveling as far afield as Los Angeles, Las Vegas, the Grand Canyon, Yellowstone National Park, and much of British Columbia and Alberta.

One memorable camping trip was to the Badlands of Alberta, an area that spans east from the town of Drumheller to the Saskatchewan border and south to the United States. It is home to the largest deposits of dinosaur bones in the world.

Driving through the dry and desert-like landscape, they came across hundreds of huge columns of rock with mushroom-like heads known as hoodoos, which had been formed by wind erosion.

Upon walking through these areas, they hoped to encounter some fossilized remains, although they were warned ahead of time not to touch or remove anything. They found it fascinating to be in a place where huge prehistoric creatures once roamed.

Continuing their journey, they proceeded west into open grassland, which was cattle country and considerably greener than the Badlands further to the east.

Their next destination was the incredibly named Smashed in Head Buffalo Jump. Not knowing the meaning of the words Buffalo Jump, they arrived at this strangely named location, drove into a large parking lot but saw nothing else.

Upon looking closer, they saw a small cliff, perhaps 35 feet high, with doors set into its face. When they entered, they found that the small cliff face had been excavated and underneath the verdant upper crust was a large museum.

What a surprise they were in for. It appeared that for over 5,000 years, the indigenous Blackfoot Indians would stampede herds of bison, craftily guiding them to the cliff's edge, where the bison would fall from the weight of the herd pressing behind them, breaking their legs and rendering them immobile. The practice, at least at this particular buffalo jump, ceased about 6,000 years ago, but the bone deposits at the foot of the jump are estimated to be 40 feet deep.

The bison thus slaughtered provided not only food but also bone with which to make tools and hide to make dwellings and clothing. According to legend, a young Blackfoot who wanted to watch the bison plunge off the cliff from below was buried under the falling animals where he had his head smashed in—hence the name.

David found the museum itself, which was opened in 1987 (he believes by Prince Charles and Lady Diana), to be absolutely incredible, giving an excellent depiction of the ecology, mythology and technology of the Blackfoot peoples of those times.

Driving back to Vancouver, Keith, Karen, Joyce and David had lots to discuss and it kept their minds occupied. Poor Sean had missed out on a real treat—by this time, he had graduated from high school and was a student at the local community college and seldom accompanied them on their camping trips.

Their camping equipment was rather basic, consisting of two tents, sleeping bags and minimal cooking equipment. Their trusty transport was the old Honda Civic purchased when they first arrived in the country. Nonetheless, they traveled far and wide and had wonderful camping holidays that provided memories that would last a lifetime.

Another such trip was a two-week holiday into the northern interior of British Columbia, where David planned to pan for gold. This really caught Keith's attention and in preparation for this pioneering endeavor, David purchased two gold pans and obtained a very old book from the library describing how to extract gold from a riverbed.

The Honda was loaded to bursting point and a friend, neighbor and mother of Keith's best friend, who frequently popped in to visit, came by to wish them bon voyage.

Once underway, their journey took them to many interesting places. They discovered some interesting camp sites where they could 'get all smoked up', an expression picked up from one of the camp site operators and which he presumed referred to the fires that all the campers made when out in the woods.

They encountered many old and derelict wooden cabins that were once inhabited by pioneers of a bygone era and wonderful clear trickling streams, way out in the vast and mountainous Canadian wilderness that screamed to David and Keith, "Here lies gold; just help yourself."

While Joyce and Karen enjoyed pottering at the camp site or bathing in the river on a hot summer day, David and Keith set to work shoveling shale from the riverbed into their gold pans, swilling and refilling them as directed in their old library book.

The sought-after thin lines of grains of gold never appeared, but according to their book, gold could also be found in the form of flakes and nuggets. To their delight, gold flakes were frequently discovered in their gold pans.

Their book on gold panning was quite specific about how to recover gold from the pan. Nuggets could be removed with tweezers and placed in a jar or bottle of river water. Thin grains and flakes of gold could be extracted from the pan by rolling them into a ball of mercury.

Being forewarned of the necessity of obtaining some mercury, David had attempted to purchase some from a pharmacy, only to be told that mercury was not for sale. Now David could recall from his schooldays how all the boys in his science class were fascinated with mercury and spent many hours literally playing with it and discovering its many incredible properties.

After several minutes of arguing with the pharmacist (which to this day he refers to as a chemist) and to the immense chagrin of the gentleman in question, he resorted to buying the four biggest thermometers in the shop.

Back at the campsite, the thermometers were destroyed and a substantial ball of mercury was obtained. However, the mercury showed no interest in collecting the gold flakes that had been painstakingly retrieved from the riverbed during the past two days.

After much head scratching and debate, they discovered that their brand-new shovel, purchased just days before the commencement of their adventure, was painted gold, and it was flakes of gold paint that they had so laboriously been collecting, not gold!

Nevertheless, the hunt continued and after several streams had been panned, their panning techniques had improved and thin lines of gold were discovered. The ball of mercury was dutifully rolled through them until it had increased considerably in size and David and Keith were ready for the next stage of their adventure.

According to their book (hereafter referred to as their bible), the next stage was to take a raw potato, cut it in two and hollow out the middle. The mercury was to be placed in the hollow, and then the potato was closed over it and sealed tightly. Following the bible's instructions to a 'T', they wired the potato closed, wrapping it in tin foil as an additional refinement and placed it on the campfire.

The theory was that, as the potato and its contents warmed, the mercury would dissipate into the potato, leaving a pristine gold nugget in the hollow. Unfortunately, nowhere in their bible did it specify when to take the potato off the fire.

With the family expectantly seated around the campfire awaiting the delivery of their first gold nugget, the potato exploded, sending fragments of gold, mercury, potato and tin foil flying in all directions. To this day, David regrets the harm and damage that his pioneering efforts caused the flora and fauna of that small portion of British Columbia.

***

In desperation at the failure of his efforts to develop Guardforce into a viable security company, he converted a section of the sporting goods store, or at least one of the window displays, into an intruder alarm installation company.

With the assistance of an East Indian acquaintance who already owned a small alarm company, he began a local advertising campaign. It succeeded in securing a few contracts but failed to develop into a viable enterprise.

Moving on to their travels once again, one exotic trip was to the Sandwich Islands, now called the Hawaiian Islands, where the famous Captain Cook was murdered by the locals and where Americans and Canadians now cavort in leis, eat roast pigs and get sunburned.

This trip was taken during the dying months of D & J Sporting Goods and should never have happened. However, it was memorable, especially the beautiful beaches where they snorkeled among schools of beautiful and colorful fish, and when they visited the incredible Polynesian Cultural Center, which depicted Hawaiians in their historical canoes and costumes.

David still has one of his oil paintings that he completed to commemorate the trip.

Meanwhile, with D & J Sports Goods sinking slowly into the mire, David called it quits, went into voluntary liquidation and, now heavily in debt, had no option but to seek employment.

Chapter Twelve

David, during a moment of navel-gazing, realized that his life so far had consisted of climbing mountains, reaching the summit and then plunging off into the deep abyss below. In England, he had thrown himself into what was then known as darkest Africa and succeeded in almost attaining the position of being the youngest inspector in the BSAP.

From there, he retired with little money to build up Sentinel Security from nothing to a force of over 50 employees before once more leaping off into another abyss, although, in this case, with some justification. Immigration to South Africa, again with little money and no prospects, became another climb, this time to reach his greatest achievement, which was to develop and eventually own the successful and highly profitable Guardforce security company.

Eager to escape the African continent, he once more hurled himself and his family off another mountaintop, expecting to enjoy another successful mountaineering achievement in Canada.

Instead, he landed with a crunch that culminated a couple of years later in becoming what he probably considered the lowest point of his life. This was no mountain climb but abject failure. No job, no money and deeply in debt.

Their very amiable landlord allowed the family to continue to live in his house despite having received no rent for two months and the bank to whom David owed a lot of money agreed to accept his 35 acres in Keremeos as partial payment of the debt and to allow David time to get his affairs in order before instituting proceedings.

What to do? David decided on two courses of action. One was to find a friend in whom he could confide and perhaps seek some comfort and guidance. The other was to go for a long walk and keep walking until he had walked off his depression and reached a solution to his problems.

Failure is not something that David took lightly nor was accustomed to, but on the plus side all three children were in school, everyone was in good health, his wife had a part-time job which, although paying only a modest salary, she banked separately and would not use to help offset the family's dire need for capital. The writing was on the wall, but David had yet to see it!

David's walk exceeded his wildest dreams and will never be forgotten. He recommends it to anyone finding themselves in dire straits and needing to shake off depression. He walked for seven or eight miles, resolving not to turn around until he had made a firm plan for his future and as he proceeded miserably westward, ideas began to take shape.

He started to cheer up and he eventually reached a decision. He would send out 20 job applications every day, negotiate the repayment of his bank loan to somewhat less than the amount owing and pay off the renegotiated amount in regular monthly installments once suitable employment had been attained. He whistled on the long walk home in a much better frame of mind.

For a very brief period, David took a job selling intruder alarms door to door. The job paid $1,000 a month plus commission. The product was useless and he didn't sell one alarm, but it put food on the table.

The Canadian World Trade Fair, Expo '86, was by this time only three or four months away and was to be held in Vancouver. The federal government was in the process of building a huge complex on Burrard Inlet on the Vancouver waterfront that would be called Canada Place, which would incorporate a large cruise ship terminal, a five-star hotel and a world trade center.

This was to be the Canadian pavilion during the Expo and would be attended by Prince Charles and Lady Diana, Princess Margaret, David's heroine British Prime Minister Margaret Thatcher, United States Vice-President George Bush and a host of other dignitaries.

Security was to be overseen by the Royal Canadian Mounted Police, but Canada's Department of Public Works was to play a huge role in implementing security measures. To this end, over 100 security guards were engaged from the large Pinkerton's security group and it was decided to employ a small group of security professionals with a variety of security experiences to enhance and oversee Pinkerton's personnel.

David was one of six persons employed for this group, which was made up of an ex-Royal Canadian Mounted Police (RCMP) woman, an ex-firefighter, a former member of the Israeli military, a former British police officer and a Scandinavian woman who had first-hand experience as a hostage and knew how a captive could slowly become empathetic with their captors, a condition known as the Stockholm syndrome.

David was still driving his little Guardforce van and Joyce still had the Honda Civic, which had taken them over so much of the North American continent.

Working for the Canadian federal government seemed to David like one big holiday. No stress or anxiety, regular hours and a regular income. He negotiated a far more reasonable settlement with his bank, paid off the debt with a series of manageable monthly payments and caught up with the house rent.

His bank manager, a Jewish gentleman with whom David was on very good terms, paid him a compliment after David made the final payment, saying, "David, I admire you, you have chutzpah," a Jewish term which David understood to mean gall, brazen nerve, effrontery and guts.

Upon reflection, he wasn't sure if this was a compliment or not, but things were looking good and he wasn't aiming to jump off any more mountain tops!

One day while at work, his tearful wife called to say that she had been involved in a traffic accident; she wasn't injured, but her little Honda Civic was a write-off.

David went to the scene of the accident to find that a woman who happened to be the wife of a local police officer had careened through a stop sign and T-boned the Honda, which had the absolute right of way.

The vehicle insurance paid out, but surprise, surprise, the policeman's wife was never prosecuted. David's wife now had no car with which to travel to and from work, so in a matter of days, they went to the local Volvo dealership and purchased a beautiful brand-new saloon. David sold the little Renault Guardforce van to help with the cost and began taking the bus to work.

When Expo '84 came to an end, the members of the Canada Place security group were disbanded, with just one exception. Just a short distance from Canada Place stood four very old six-story buildings owned by the federal government that occupied a complete city block.

These buildings were undergoing a 40 million dollar renovation, which would not only modernize the government office space but would turn the two lower levels into a retail mall with a glass-covered atrium.

The exception was David, who was made a fully-fledged employee of the federal government and was required to organize and implement manpower and electronic security for the soon-to-become Sinclair Center. In order to comply with government requirements, David became a Canadian citizen—his third citizenship after the British and Rhodesian citizenships.

All of the office space was occupied by numerous federal government departments and the hunt was on to find tenants for the 100,000 square feet of retail space. Much of this work was done before David arrived on the scene. A large corner of the center was taken by a very exclusive and expensive Italian clothing store and a food court was quickly leased to a variety of fast-food chains.

David, who had already completed the security design and installation, was given the task of leasing and managing the retail mall, in addition to overseeing security, with a considerable improvement in salary.

With finances again in the black, it was decided that it was time to buy a house. The money that Joyce had scrupulously been saving was used as a down payment and a rather unusual two-story, four-bedroom Tyrolean-styled home was purchased in North Vancouver. David continued taking the bus to work, while Joyce used the new Volvo to get to work and back.

***

Taking the opportunity to travel in the new and rather prestigious Volvo, David decided to take the family down to San Diego, camping along the way at Lake Havasu to see the old London Bridge, the bridge that he had seen being dismantled in 1969, in its new location, and to visit Las Vegas.

They found the bridge and walked over its hallowed archways, but the dry heat of the Arizona desert was stifling. Keith and Karen soon spotted an isolated ice cream parlor nearby and quickly headed for it. Upon entering, they found that it was completely air-conditioned.

Air conditioning was very uncommon in Canada, but in Arizona, with temperatures well in excess of 100 degrees, it was a godsend. They each bought their favorite ice cream cone and quickly demolished it, but going outside again into the blistering heat after the air-conditioned luxury of the ice cream parlor was more than they could take, so back inside they went to order another ice cream.

After a hasty retreat to the Volvo, they set off for Las Vegas. With no air conditioning and with all the car windows open—it was a Canadian car, remember—they gradually cooled down and upon arriving in Las Vegas, set up camp in a KOA campground on the city outskirts.

This was David's first visit to Las Vegas and all the glitz and glamour were something of a surprise. He noticed several billboards advertising cash for cars and jewelry but thought no more of it until he saw one gentleman, smartly dressed in a suit and tie, filling people's cars at a gas station. Obviously, the poor sucker had gambled all his money, car and wristwatch away and was trying to earn a few dollars to pay for his fare home.

Keith was monumentally displeased when deposited at a local MacDonald's with his sister, while Mom and Dad tried their luck at the slot machines at a casino just across the street. Needless to say, they weren't there very long before they'd blown the 40 or 50 dollars that they had allowed themselves. Then it was back to the camp site for their onward journey to San Diego.

David was very impressed with San Diego. The climate and the beaches were wonderful, the cleanliness and the landscaping were some of the best he'd ever seen and their visit to the San Diego Zoo was incredible. With over 3,000 animals, many in open air, cageless exhibits that recreated the animal's natural habitat, it was without question exceptional.

They took the long drive back to Vancouver, satisfied with yet another camping trip under their belts. The only downside was that David had forgotten his wristwatch in the San Diego campsite restroom.

Life was definitely getting better. David was enjoying his job and, because of his increasing involvement with the management of Sinclair Center's office space, was urged to become a certified property manager (CPM) with the Building Owners and Managers Association (BOMA), which he did.

With the help of two ladies with previous shopping center experience, the shopping mall's retail space became fully leased and the center was a growing success. A baby grand piano was installed in the atrium and used by a variety of local pianists every lunch hour. Mall promotions became a large part of David's responsibility.

As a government employee, David was automatically required to become a union member.

He wasn't all that impressed with union tactics, firstly with the stevedores' performance at the Southampton docks, and secondly after seeing a recent post office strike in Canada, where he witnessed postal workers hurling bags of mail out of trucks onto the public highway to be blown to all points of the wind— mail that people had paid to be delivered and that contained a multitude of important documents, checks and private correspondence.

His union decided to strike for higher wages and better working conditions, which David considered a joke. He viewed many of his colleagues as lazy incompetents, but nonetheless they picketed all federal government buildings, including the Sinclair Center.

Arriving for work on the first morning of the strike, he found the building surrounded by several hundred striking workers waving placards and yelling on bullhorns. They blocked all entrances to the center, which meant that the public could not gain access to the retail shops.

David, much to the chagrin of his fellow government workers, forced his way in and met with his irate retail tenants. The mall was empty, the food court was empty, and David proposed a course of action that created mixed reactions in the days to come.

He obtained large sheets of cardboard and some sticks and felt-tipped pens and organized his retail tenants to make placards, stating, "The retail mall in Sinclair Center is open for business. Don't be intimidated."

David then led them outside where they marched with the pickets, gaining much abuse from them and much praise from passing motorists.

Members of the public began breaking the picket line, especially those accustomed to taking their lunch in the center's food court, and of course the media, in the form of TV, radio and newspaper reporters, were in attendance.

The media interviewed several of these demonstrators, including David, and he was asked specifically, "Aren't you a member of the union?" and "Why are you not joining the pickets?"

His answers were a direct 'Yes' to the first and a more complex "I'm between a rock and a hard place with a lot of empathy for our retail tenants," response to the second.

His comments were broadcast nationwide on TV and his regional department head stated that 'Bird will be fired for this' or words to that effect.

The following day, there were no pickets at Sinclair Center, but a press release from the union stated that because of the mixed-use nature of the center plus the negative public response to the previous day's events, union members would no longer picket Sinclair Center.

Several hundred did however congregate in the large parking area on the opposite side of the street and when David, in his role as head of security, appeared on the roof of the building to assess the situation first-hand, a huge roar erupted with constant shouts of 'Jump, jump, jump'.

David subsequently received much praise for his actions and was never fired or admonished. However, he did become less than popular with many of his colleagues.

It was around this time that David began receiving small payments from his bank account in Rhodesia or, more correctly, Zimbabwe. The Zimbabwean currency had devalued considerably since 1967 and the Canadian bank made a charge for converting every payment into Canadian currency.

It finally reached a point when the bank phoned David, telling him that their charge exceeded the amount of the payment. From there on, the Zimbabwean dollar became so ridiculously devalued that it cost somewhere in the region of a million Zimbabwean dollars to buy a loaf of bread!

***

In the summer of 1990, David's sister and their mother, by then well into her eighties, visited them in Vancouver. It was a wonderful time with lots to chat about. At some point, David mentioned that there was a street in West Vancouver named Ronayne Road, which was of course Rose's maiden name.

Much had been made of the Ronaynes over the years and David's cousin had done a tremendous amount of research. The Ronaynes were a well-known family in County Cork, Southern Ireland, predominantly in the small town of Youghal, where, until recently, their large house had stood.

It appeared that back in the mid- to late-1800s, a black sheep of the family had been banned and sent to England where he married a French Huguenot woman. Several generations later, Rose and her two sisters arrived on the scene.

It was always rumored that the French woman, whose maiden name was Agumbar, came from a wealthy family and that a small fortune remained 'in chancery' somewhere in France for legitimate descendants to claim. No one ever did, but the thought was always at the back of David's mind.

Linda and her brother John had been to the British Museum and were, after donning white cotton gloves, given one hour in which to examine a rare book describing the family history of the Ronaynes. John painstakingly drew a copy of the Ronayne coat of arms, while Linda scanned through the pages frantically scribbling notes.

David again mentioned that there was a Ronayne Road in West Vancouver and took his mother to see it. She was suitably impressed and had her photograph taken beneath the sign. Then, a short trip to the West Vancouver library revealed that several Ronaynes lived in the small British Columbian town of Pemberton.

A few days later, the family packed a picnic lunch and drove the 100 miles north to Pemberton where, sure enough, they discovered a small graveyard several miles beyond Pemberton village where many Ronaynes were buried. This was a revelation to Rose.

Apart from her father and his immediate family, she had never come across a Ronayne or any reference to the family in the almost 90 years that she had lived in England.

Photographs were taken and they were headed home when David noticed the name Ronayne on a mailbox nailed to a farmyard gate. A man was driving a tractor on the farm and David asked him for more information. The man told him to visit his sister, who had done considerable research into the Ronayne family of County Cork. She lived in Pemberton and they were given directions.

They found the house with no difficulty and the sister, whose maiden name was Ronayne, answered the door. When she met Mom and heard her story, she welcomed them all in for tea and fascinated everyone by the telling of her research.

She then produced a book on the history of the Ronaynes, which, to Linda's absolute astonishment, was the same book that she and John had seen in the British Museum.

Rosemary offered to have the entire contents of the book photocopied and after Linda and Mom had returned to England, David made several more copies, had them bound into books and presented one to each of the Ronayne sisters.

During late 1990 or early 1991, with the 1992 Olympic Games in Spain approaching, David incorporated a series of Spanish entertainments into the mall's promotion campaign. The sounds of castanets and stomping feet filled the air and a very generous donation of two round trip airline tickets to Barcelona by British Airways provided a grand prize for one lucky raffle-prize winner.

When David first telephoned British Airways to ask if they would donate tickets to the raffle, he spoke with their manager for western Canada. The gentleman had a very plummy British accent and agreed to meet with David at the Sinclair Center to discuss the matter further.

When they met, David was astounded because his British counterpart was, in fact, an East Indian from the state of Goa. The man had an incredible history with British Airways dating back to his very first job with them as a baggage handler at Goa's airport and credited his mother, who was a teacher of English, for impressing upon him the importance of speaking the queen's English. David had found a new friend.

Chapter Thirteen

Mom and Linda were transported to the airport for their return journey home after what David believed was a wonderful visit. However, on the drive home from the airport, Joyce said that they had to talk.

Totally puzzled, David took her aside to ask what this talk was about and was told that she was leaving him, had a small apartment in West Vancouver in mind and had consulted a lawyer.

Their silver wedding anniversary was 14 May, 1991 but there was no celebration. Their house was on the market and an amicable decision was made as to the division of property and assets.

Karen, then ten, was to stay with her mother. Keith, then seventeen and finishing his final year of high school, was to stay with David. Sean, then 23, had had enough and was in an apartment in North Vancouver and had a very good job with the Sony Corporation. Once the house was sold, Joyce moved out symbolically on Valentine's Day, 1992!

It was during this traumatic period in David's life that he was diagnosed with diabetes brought on by stress, according to his doctor. David was not overweight and there was no history of diabetes in his family, so he concluded that the stress was brought on by the break-up of the family, which was absolutely devastating to him. Thank you very much!

Once the house had been sold, assets split up and his wife and Karen ensconced in their rented apartment in West Vancouver, David and Keith moved into a two-bedroom townhouse in North Vancouver.

David had no means of transport as the Volvo had been part of his wife's share of their assets, but by taking a 30-minute walk, David could catch the sea-bus across Burrard Inlet to his work in downtown Vancouver. Keith was to complete his twelfth grade at West Vancouver High School and graduate in the summer of 1992.

Now a bachelor, one of David's problems was what he and Keith were going to eat. Apart from the odd *braivleis* or barbecue he had never cooked, so enlisting the aid of young Karen, he had her write out some of her mother's recipes and she dutifully produced four—namely, shepherd's pie, bangers and mash, curry and rice and spaghetti bolognaise. That is what they lived on for the next few months.

On one of his evenings out having a few beers with his posh-speaking British Airways East Indian friend, David happened to mention his visits to the British Middle East Sporting and Dining Club in Durban and their wonderful curries.

Incredibly, his friend had visited Durban and knew of the restaurant and as the discussion progressed, he learned two important things. One was that you can never put too many onions in an East African curry and the other was to use curry paste rather than curry powder, as the latter tends to give the curry a somewhat metallic taste.

On many occasions since that discussion, David has made curries, usually beef curry, and always to the amazement and delight of the recipients. For those who may be interested, here is the recipe:

First, cut up one pound of stewing beef into small pieces removing all fat, skin and gristle and lightly brown it in a pot. Add previously chopped onions (three), tomatoes (three), potato (one), celery (two sticks) and carrot (one). Once it reaches a light boil, stir in several tablespoons of Patak's Madras curry paste. Remember that the more you add, the hotter the curry. Simmer at a very low boil for 90 minutes, then allow to cool and refrigerate overnight.

Before serving the following day, prepare the sambals and rice. Jasmine rice usually takes 20 minutes and should be flavored/colored with turmeric and be fairly loose and crumbly when served.

David's sambals usually consist of unsweetened coconut, crushed pecans, finely chopped onion and tomato, sultanas (generally known in North America as golden raisins), sliced banana and mango chutney, preferably Mrs. Ball's chutney from South Africa.

The resultant curry, obviously heated after a night in the fridge, poured over a bed of rice and liberally smothered with sambals, will result in an exceptional meal, especially if accompanied by a pint of Worthington 'E' if you can find it.

Now, what was he going to do with the rest of his life?

Well, the first thing he did after his separation was to buy a bicycle and almost every evening after work, he rode five miles through heavy traffic to visit Karen. She was always a daddy's girl and they did, and still do, thoroughly enjoy each other's company.

Losing his family was tragic to David and as one who tends to hold onto grudges for a long, long time, it's unlikely that he will ever forget or forgive his wife's actions. He filed for divorce after a twelve-month separation and has seen almost nothing of his ex-wife since.

The second thing that David did prove beyond a shadow of a doubt that all the rumors circulating about male menopause and a man's tendency to go sideways into a full-blown mid-life crisis are false (tongue in cheek). Within weeks of becoming single, he joined a singles club that hosted regular social evenings.

He decided that a new beginning was in order and that he would start a new life. He was certainly no loner and finding an attractive mate was his quest. A wonderful woman soon came into his life and made him feel young again—no mean feat at the age of 47. They were together for almost 18 months and would have eventually wed had not the future held other plans.

Step three was to solve the transportation issue and to this end he purchased an 850cc Suzuki shaft-drive motorcycle, complete with panniers and fairing. The bike gave him a sense of freedom and both Karen and his paramour enjoyed being pillion passengers.

Step four, several months later, was to purchase an ageing and somewhat dilapidated Ford Mustang, which rounded out the transportation issues, especially on those all-too-frequent rainy days when the motorcycle was impractical.

Step five was the purchase of a 30-foot Catalina sailboat moored at Eagle Harbor in West Vancouver. Although small, it was a four-berth boat with an outboard motor and a tiller rather than a wheel. The only sailing experience David ever had was in his small mirror dinghy and a few outings on a friend's Fireball sailing dinghy in South Africa.

The Scotsman who sold him the Catalina became a good friend and gave him some rudimentary lessons on how to sail. Thereafter, David learned by trial and error, taking the boat out single-handed most weekends and sometimes finding a small cove in which to anchor and spend the night.

At about this time, David was well into his career as a shopping center manager and attended a shopping center conference in Nashville, Tennessee as a member of the International Council of Shopping Centers.

Staying at the Opryland Hotel was an experience in itself, with its hundreds of rooms, the large expanse of beautifully landscaped grounds and several restaurants and constant live country and western performances.

While in Nashville, David couldn't miss the opportunity to visit the Grand Ole Opry and, during an evening performance, saw the famous Canadian country singer Hank Snow in one of his last performances ever, and also an up-and-coming newcomer named Vince Gill. Out with the old and in with the new, as the saying goes.

Once the conference was over, David checked out of the hotel the following morning, suitably dressed for his flight back to Vancouver that evening. With nothing much to do, he asked the taxi driver to take him where he could purchase cowboy boots, thinking that they would be a nice memento of his visit and very practical when riding his motorcycle.

The taxi driver obliged, dropping him and his suitcase off at a street that was full of shops selling country- and western-type regalia. Almost every one sold boots and several had boots on sale. David selected a suitable emporium and, after a discussion with a shop assistant, was presented with a selection of cowboy boots.

The salesman, realizing that David was totally ignorant on the subject of cowboy boots, went to great lengths to explain that the perfectly fitting boot was rather tight to put on but that once the heel popped in and the toes had some wriggle room, it would be the perfect fit.

Assisted by the salesman, several boots were tried on until David's feet, just like Cinderella's slipper, just popped in and felt comfortable. David decided to purchase the boots, but rather than put them in his suitcase, he chose to wear them on the journey home and placed his regular shoes in his suitcase.

This way, he figured, he would avoid having to declare his purchase to the customs official when entering Canada.

He then caught a taxi to the airport, feeling at least an inch taller in his new boots and enjoying the sensation. He checked in and bid farewell to his suitcase as it disappeared on the conveyor belt behind the check-in desk.

After enjoying a couple of beers in the airport lounge, it was time to board the plane for the six-hour flight to Vancouver and with an interesting book to pass the time, he was looking forward to returning home.

During the flight, as usually happened during a long flight, his feet began to swell and became uncomfortable. He realized that he should have thought of this before hastily deciding to wear the boots on the way home but ignored the discomfort and focused on reading his book.

After about four hours of flying time, the pilot informed the passengers that due to severely inclement weather in Vancouver, their aircraft would be diverted to Seattle, where they would be accommodated in a local hotel and returned to SeaTac airport early the following morning for the remainder of their flight to Vancouver.

David began worrying about his uncomfortable feet, but at least he would be able to get his damned boots off and enjoy a few hours' sleep.

The passengers were conveyed to a rather seedy hotel on the outskirts of Seattle but did not have access to their luggage. It was around midnight by this time and everyone was anxious to get to their rooms for some shuteye. David was no exception.

Once in his room, he flopped down on the bed to remove his boots, but they wouldn't budge. As much as he twisted and turned, there was no way he could grip the boots to pull them off and without taking his boots off he couldn't take his trousers off. In desperation, he lay on the floor, opened the door and with his other foot clamped the heel of his boot between the door and the door jamb.

After a hell of a struggle and a lot of pain, he eventually removed one boot and the skin from his instep. Repeating the procedure caused the loss of skin from his other instep, more pain and a significant amount of blood on the thin ankle socks that he was wearing.

Relieved of the damned boots, he fell into a deep and welcome sleep, only to be awoken at about four in the morning and told that an early breakfast was being served for passengers being bussed to the airport.

In alarm, he realized that he would now have to put the damned boots back on if he wanted to catch his plane. He did so—trousers first, then boots, scraping his skinless insteps in the process before hobbling down to the breakfast room.

What his fellow passengers must have thought was anyone's guess, but he imagined that they must have thought that he'd had one hell of a night.

On arrival at Vancouver airport, he hobbled through customs and excise, thinking how happily he would have parted with the duty on a pair of unused cowboy boots instead of enduring the misery of the past 24 hours.

Upon hearing of his escapades with the boots when he arrived home, the lady he was living with asked why the salesman didn't include a boot jack with the sale.

"A boot jack? What's a boot jack?"

It turned out that a boot jack is a simple piece of wood elevated at one end, with a hollowed-out end at the other that allows the wearer to step on it while slotting the heel of the other boot into the hollow and gently removing foot from boot. Simple!

Ever since that unfortunate incident, any time David hears the word Nashville, it sends a shudder down his spine. Anyone want to buy a pair of genuine, hardly used Nashville cowboy boots?

***

On the sporting scene, in view of Vancouver's unpredictable and inclement weather, David decided to take up the indoor racket sport of squash and played a few regular games every week with a newfound friend from work, Jerry. David was no better at squash than he had been at tennis but had a good workout chasing the infernally small and lackluster ball around the court.

With transport and recreation sorted out and a good job with the federal government secured, David felt that his life was back on track. Work was going well and the Sinclair Center was fully leased.

In fact, the center won an award for the promotion held earlier that featured the Barcelona Olympic Games. An award that was to be presented at the Waldorf Astoria Hotel later that year in New York in combination with a shopping center convention, a convention that he was going to attend and which resulted in life-changing consequences.

Earlier that year, David had attended a course at Michigan State University on shopping center management coupled with an examination to obtain his CSM (Certified Shopping Center Manager) with the International Council of Shopping Center's.

He and five other shopping center managers from British Columbia studied for the exam for a year and all six headed for Michigan State University's Kellogg Center in East Lansing, Michigan. Out of the six, he was the only one who succeeded in passing.

While in this course, David met a woman who managed commercial properties in Fort Lauderdale, Florida—a woman who also gained her CSM certification and who was to change David's life forever!

Chapter Fourteen

Bonnie was charming, attractive and a couple of years younger than David. Florida born and bred, she was an avid scuba diver and a successful businesswoman who lived in Pompano Beach, which is a relatively small town just north of Fort Lauderdale.

David was surprised to find her so un-American. She wasn't loud or flashy, but underneath her very modest and quiet exterior was an interesting and intelligent individual. David told her that she 'hid her light under a bushel' and that holds true to this day. What Bonnie made of David, he still hasn't figured out.

Whatever the reason, they hit it off from the moment they met and they stayed in contact via telephone and snail mail. Bonnie would also be attending the shopping center convention in New York, so that would be their second opportunity to meet.

As things turned out, it transpired that their meeting at Michigan State University must have been love at first sight for after their second meeting in New York it was decided that Bonnie would sell her house, give up her job and move to Vancouver where they would wed. This was no small decision, considering that Bonnie hadn't lived outside the U.S. before.

The next step was for Bonnie to put her house on the market and pay a visit to Vancouver. David also had the task of obtaining and furnishing some accommodation, as he had been staying with his lady-friend since Keith had moved out of their first dwelling over a year earlier and moved into a shared basement suite with his brother Sean.

David's need to find a permanent place to live was accentuated by the fact that Bonnie was due to arrive on Labor Day, just a few weeks away.

He moved out of his lady-friend's residence and took up temporary lodgings on the floor of Keith and Sean's shared basement suite. He soon succeeded in finding a small apartment in North Vancouver and following a rapid purchase he furnished and prepared his small garden apartment in what he thought was a modern but minimalist style.

Bonnie flew into Seattle's SeaTac airport on her first visit, arriving on Labor Day in 1993. David drove his Mustang down to Washington state and waited patiently at the gate as passengers poured through, but there was no sign of Bonnie. Oh, no! Was this another mountain he'd just jumped off? Then, there she was, dragging her suitcase behind her—probably the last piece of luggage off the plane.

From this point onwards, they had a wonderful week together, sailing at the weekend, sightseeing on the motorcycle and, best of all, spending time with Sean, Keith and especially twelve-year-old Karen. Bonnie didn't have children and here she was taking on a whole family.

David often tells of Bonnie's reaction to his newly acquired apartment. Apparently, his minimalist approach to furnishings, particularly to crockery and cutlery, which basically consisted of two plates, two cups and saucers, two knives, forks and spoons, didn't cut the mustard.

Bonnie's house took longer than anticipated to sell and immigration formalities had to be completed so for almost a year their long-distance romance was kept alive by alternative monthly flights to either Seattle or Fort Lauderdale.

Finally, during the summer of 1994, Bonnie's house sold, she resigned from her job in Fort Lauderdale and her immigration documents arrived with a proviso that she married David within six months of her arrival.

David flew south to meet up with Bonnie and they drove almost 4,000 miles to Vancouver in her Toyota Cressida, which thankfully would replace David's tired Mustang. The journey took one week and provided a wonderful opportunity to visit many landmarks, which included Mount Rushmore, Yellowstone National Park and the little-known town of Ten Sleep in Wyoming, which had the sweetest water they had ever tasted.

For those readers who have never visited Ten Sleep, the reason for its unlikely name originates from native Indians, specifically the Shoshones and the Crows. It was the crossroads from which it took ten sleeps to reach either reservation.

In compliance with Bonnie's immigration requirements, it was decided that their wedding would be a civil ceremony and would take place on a small wooden bridge in a park on the waterfront in West Vancouver on New Year's Eve in 1994.

The only people present would be the Commissioner of Oaths to conduct the ceremony and David's squash partner Jerry and his wife to bear witness. Thereafter, they would adjourn to a local restaurant to celebrate. Not another soul would know.

That evening, to celebrate the New Year, David and Bonnie were hosting a New Year's Eve party in their tiny garden apartment. Approximately 20 guests arrived and at midnight they announced that they were now man and wife. Their guests were incredulous, especially Karen, Keith and Sean, but all were delighted to hear the news. It was a day that they were never to forget, for how could one forget a wedding anniversary on New Year's Eve!

The one-bedroom apartment in North Vancouver was later sold in favor of a much nicer two-bedroom townhouse in the suburb of Coquitlam. Bonnie gained employment as the manager of a shopping mall in New Westminster.

David continued to make progress in managing all the commercial properties owned by the federal government, taking control of retail operations across Canada. In addition, they still had the security company, although it had now dwindled to just one contract with the same two employees.

During the course of his period as manager of government-owned commercial properties, David made several business trips to Ottawa, Montreal and Quebec City. Ottawa, the capital city of Canada and its political center, has an outdoor pedestrian mall known as Sparks Street, which features a number of restaurants and retail stores.

Nearly all of these commercial properties were owned and managed by the federal government and thus fell under David's area of responsibility. He became familiar with the street and would frequently fly to Ottawa. Sparks Street was at one time the home of a number of government offices and homes for parliamentarians, but it later became Ottawa's commercial hub.

During the mid-twentieth century, most of the government-occupied offices were moved out, the street was closed to traffic and although still predominantly owned by the federal government, the area was turned into a pedestrian mall with a primarily commercial occupancy.

Visits to Montreal were less frequent, but David found the city fascinating, especially its underground city, which due to Montreal's inclement weather, is set in interconnected complexes above and below ground and extends for almost 20 miles. It is full of shops and restaurants, even theaters, offering over 600,000 square feet of retail space.

Of the three cities, David claims that the jewel in the crown should go to Old Quebec City. Designated as a World Heritage Site in 1985, Old Quebec is the most intact fortified town north of Mexico, retaining its 400-year-old colonial architecture.

Its history goes back four centuries and it thrived for 150 years as a French colony before the British takeover in 1759. Under Britain, Old Quebec continued to function as a bastion, this time against the continuing threat of invasion by the United States.

David visited the nearby extraordinary site overlooking the Plains of Abraham, where on 13 September 1759, the Battle of the Plains of Abraham took place between the French and the British. When he visited the Plains, it had been converted to a park that received some 4 million tourists and visitors annually for sports, relaxation and outdoor concerts.

***

Back in Vancouver, their sailboat, which was now named *Geronimo* in honor of Bonnie's leap of faith, was becoming something of a hindrance. Moorage was costly, the boat needed major restoration and there seemed very little time to make use of it, so the decision was made to sell.

The sale of *Geronimo* was undertaken by the sales office at the marina and David and Bonnie were off on their travels when the sale occurred. Upon their return, they were notified that the sale had been completed and David went to the marina to collect his check.

Geronimo, as the reader may recall, had a small outboard engine that was used to motor in and out of the marina and this motor tended to misbehave from time to time.

It transpired that on the day of the sale, two somewhat shady and slightly inebriated characters came to the marina, purchased the boat with cash, and told the staff that they intended to sail to Seattle that very day.

They then asked directions and were told to head out of the marina on the motor directly toward a small island about a half mile offshore where they could set the sails, turn to port and head south.

According to the marina staff, all went well except that *Geronimo* failed to turn to port and instead plowed straight into the island, where it grounded and remained stranded. Shortly afterwards, the Coast Guard arrived on the scene, put the two sailors in handcuffs and hauled *Geronimo* back to the marina where, to the best of David's knowledge, it remains to this day.

***

Accompanied by Bonnie, David's next shopping center convention took place in New Orleans, a city that David had never visited before. He found the downtown area, particularly the French quarter, remarkably different from other places that he had visited in the United States.

Yes, there were plenty of Americans, Black and white, and the city struck him as very cosmopolitan. There were also many tourists from all over the world and with a lot of heavy drinking and noise going on, the atmosphere was jovial and lively.

As a traditional jazz fan, David was eager to visit Preservation Hall, a famous jazz venue on St. Peter Street in the French quarter. He was fascinated to find that it was, at least back in the nineties, a rundown old hall with creaky wooden floorboards and no seats apart from an old wooden bench at the back, which was fully occupied.

Sitting on the floor with a couple of dozen other people, they were treated to a fantastic couple of hours of pure, unadulterated traditional jazz by five Black musicians playing saxophone, clarinet, double bass, banjo and drums. What a treat.

David and Bonnie, later met up with an old friend of David's and the three of them retired to a nearby café for drinks and a snack. The café was empty except for three men sitting at the table next to them, and after a while the lady who was with them whispered to Bonnie that one of the men was Pete Townsend, co-founder, leader, principal songwriter and guitarist of the rock band, The Who.

David had never heard of Pete Townsend or the Who, having spent most of the 60s and 70s in darkest Africa, but the girls had and were all of a twitter. He must have noticed, for he came over and adorned each of them with a few cheap and gaudy necklaces, apparently another New Orleans tradition that David was unaware of.

Travel became of great interest to both David and Bonnie and although David had lived in four countries on three different continents, Bonnie had never been overseas and was anxious to broaden her horizons. Their first trip overseas after getting married was to England, where Bonnie met David's mother, brother John and Sister Linda, as well as many cousins. David's father had passed away some years previously at the age of 82.

David, usually accompanied by either his brother or sister, took great pleasure in taking Bonnie to various English landmarks.

They visited Stonehenge; Bonnie stood on the spot at the Tower of London where Anne Boleyn was beheaded; and they went to Trafalgar Square and onto the Royal Navy's flagship, *HMS Victory* at Portsmouth, where a plaque marking the very spot where Lord Horatio Nelson died at the Battle of Trafalgar, is prominently displayed.

Bonnie also saw some of southern England's beautiful countryside, narrow country lanes and quaint villages and pubs.

They visited Britain several times thereafter and on one occasion drove to the small village of Lacock in Wiltshire, just outside the Cotswolds. David had never been there before and was amazed at this incredibly quaint, historic and, thanks to the National Trust, a well-preserved example of 'Olde' England. In one of the pubs stood a huge stone fireplace with a spit big enough to turn an ox.

The spit, amazingly still in place, disappeared through the immense fireplace wall and was attached on the other side to a large wooden wheel similar to the wheels seen in hamster cages. According to the publican, in the days of yore when the spit was in use, a small dog, a breed predictably enough called a turnspit, was put to running inside the wheel, thus turning the roast as it cooked over the fire.

The publican would have at least two of these dogs so that they could run in shifts.

The turnspit was a short-legged, long-bodied dog specifically bred and trained to run on the wheel. This breed of dog is now extinct but is mentioned in the 1576 edition of the book *Of English Dogs* under the name 'Turnespete' and again in William Bingley's *Memoirs of British Quadrupeds* (1809).

***

Back in Florida, Bonnie's mother lived in a magnificent old house in the small coastal town of Port Orange, close to the motor racing city of Daytona Beach. The house, built in 1924, was located on a one-acre waterfront lot and had been Bonnie's family home since 1961. With a large swimming pool, wrap-around porch and a multitude of bedrooms and garages, it was the envy of the neighborhood.

Bonnie's father had passed away several years previously and David had never met him. They were frequent visitors to Port Orange because Bonnie's mother, who was in failing health, was becoming increasingly dependent on Bonnie's twin brother and a granddaughter who lived nearby.

The nearby city of Daytona Beach is a mecca for motorcyclists and every year, during the month of March, it plays host to Bike Week. An event that has been staged there for over 80 years.

Literally, tens of thousands of motorcyclists descend on the city, where their main focus is on Main Street and the delights to be had there. Scantily clad women offer a bike wash and there are plenty of bars and restaurants, one of which is situated opposite an old cemetery and is called The Boot Hill Saloon. A humorous sign at the front entrance reads, "Come on in, grab a seat. You're better off here than across the street."

The roar of motorcycle engines drowns out the sound of gentle waves lapping against the sandy shore and many folks leave town until it's over. However, Bike Week brings a lot of revenue into town and for that, the citizens are truly grateful.

***

In mid-1997, David and Bonnie took another trip to England, this time taking Keith and Karen with them and on 21 June there was a family reunion in Bedhampton to celebrate David's mother's ninetieth birthday. A nearby hall was rented, catering and liquid refreshment organized and the entire affair went off splendidly.

A couple of days later, David rented a car and the four of them headed off to Portsmouth, where they boarded a ferry to Le Havre in France. The first stop was Paris, where they visited the Eiffel Tower, the Arc de Triomphe and many other favorite tourist hot spots.

Driving a British, right-hand drive car through France proved something of a challenge, especially in Paris, as they all drove on the 'wrong' side of the road. They then headed south to Cannes and the French Riviera, where they had a splendid time touring several beachside towns along that beautiful Mediterranean coastline.

From the Riviera, they drove through the Camargue region to the city of Arles in the Provence-Alpes-Côte d'Azur region. A third of the Camargue consists of lakes or wetlands. It is home to more than 400 species of birds and its brine ponds are one of the few European habitats for the flamingo. It is also unique for its breed of white horses and for breeding fighting bulls for export to Spain.

David was incredulous at finding a huge Roman amphitheater in the city of Arles. The amphitheater, built in 90 A.D., holds 20,000 people and was used by the Romans for chariot races and bloody hand-to-hand battles. More recently, it has been used for bullfighting as well as for concerts and plays.

Another surprise was that when he was seated in an outdoor café, he noticed that next to him was the café painted by Vincent Van Gogh and named *Café Terrace at Night*. And he was seated in the very same spot where Van Gogh must have set up his easel back in 1888. Wonderful.

Eventually, everyone had to return to Bedhampton, but they all agreed that it had been an eye-opening experience.

***

The following year, David, now aged 53, was becoming concerned about rumblings at head office that the privatization of some of the management of government-owned properties was being contemplated and he began looking into the possibility of taking early retirement on a reduced pension.

At the same time, his own health, specifically his diabetes, was slowly deteriorating despite rigorous and regular games of squash.

He began running regularly after returning home from work and what started as a one- or two-mile jog eventually evolved into nightly runs of ten or twelve miles. He began losing weight, found himself more alert and realized that running would probably be beneficial in his battle with diabetes.

After much deliberation, David decided to apply for early retirement from the federal government at the end of 1999, at which time he would have turned

55 and would move to Florida where Bonnie could take care of her mother. This inspired David to intensify his interest in painting, focus more on his running and dispose of his motorcycle.

David had seen many motorcyclists when visiting Florida and noted that most of them were old and fat. He didn't want to emulate them and decided that the bike must go.

The specialist treating his diabetes was encouraged by his running, but when he announced that he intended to run the London marathon in early 1999, she thought it was just a pipe dream. That was like throwing down the gauntlet and he increased his nightly runs to fifteen or sixteen miles.

***

David had a very special friend with whom he had served in the British South Africa Police, the previously mentioned New Zealander predictably named Kiwi, who had since returned to New Zealand. Kiwi and his wife were well established in the small town of Cambridge on the north island and invited David and Bonnie to visit them.

The motorcycle was subsequently crated up and shipped to Auckland, from where they would tour New Zealand and then sell the bike before returning home. Arrangements were made and during a fierce snowstorm on Christmas Eve 1998, they left Vancouver and flew to Singapore for a three-night stopover before flying on to Auckland.

Surprisingly, during their flight to Singapore, they crossed the international dateline and landed in Singapore on Boxing Day. Where did Christmas Day go?

Singapore proved to be a delightful surprise. The city was spotlessly clean, with strict laws prohibiting expectorating in public and the sale of chewing gum. Christmas decorations were everywhere and every public washroom they visited had an attendant present to ensure that the facility was kept clean.

A drink at the famous Raffles Hotel long bar was a delightful treat and David discovered that they still served yards and half-yards of ale. They enjoyed visiting Singapore's huge botanical gardens and the magnificent orchid house as well as the Bugis Street Market.

What an experience this huge market was, selling everything from fresh meat and fish, clothing and trinkets to several fine dining restaurants, trendy cafes and bars. You just name it and it's there. They spent hours just walking through this fully enclosed market, amazed at the variety of goods on sale.

Another thing that surprised David were the numerous jeweler's shops displaying magnificent gold necklaces, rings and bracelets. This was no doubt due to the large Indian population, with its special penchant for gold, that occupied the island.

As promised, Kiwi was at the airport in Auckland to meet them and transport them to the warehouse where their motorcycle was being stored. It was uncrated, none the worse for wear, filled with petrol and the battery connected.

It started like a dream. Before heading to Cambridge, which is about 100 miles south of Auckland, they followed Kiwi on a short tour of the city, which included a ride to the top of One Tree Hill, where they had a magnificent view of the City of Sails below. Sadly, shortly after their visit, vandals destroyed the single tree that gave the hill its name.

From there, it was on to Cambridge, where they were warmly greeted by Kiwi's family and treated to a barbecue and refreshments followed by a wonderful evening catching up on old times.

The following month consisted of touring New Zealand's North Island to visit its hot springs, the Horn of Plenty, the 90-mile beach and Cape Reinga, where the Tasmanian Sea meets the Pacific Ocean. The New Zealanders were very friendly and hospitable, especially when they saw the motorcycle's British Columbia license plates; the roads were narrow, winding and perfect for motorcycling and their summer weather was fantastic.

On New Year's Eve, the last day of 1998 and their 4th wedding anniversary, they found themselves in Rotorua in the Bay of Plenty, New Zealand's twelfth-largest city. It is known for its geothermal activity and features hot mud pools and hot springs, and David and Bonnie both enjoyed having a hot spring water massage.

In the evening, there was a well-attended fireworks display and plenty of restaurants with sidewalk seating where they participated in one of their favorite pastimes, people watching!

Touring the northern half of New Zealand's North Island ensured that they enjoyed warm summer weather but it deprived them of the opportunity to see the majestic beauty further south. This was probably a mistake, but something to add to David's bucket list for future travels.

***

Upon returning home from their New Zealand trip at the beginning of 1999, it was determined that the government was indeed intent on handing over management of its commercial properties to the private sector, so David's application to take early retirement at age 55 was approved and his last day of work would be New Year's Eve of 1999.

Bonnie and David's 5th wedding anniversary with only three months to go before heading off to England for the London marathon, David's training became even more intense, and he was now running distances of up to 20 miles every evening after work.

When marathon day arrived, David, Bonnie, Sister Linda and brother John all went up to the Docklands on the River Thames, where competitors were to congregate before taking transport to Greenwich, the starting point for the race. At this point, David was left with thousands of runners, some of whom were dressed in the most ridiculous costumes.

Men wearing tutus, people in clown outfits and even one couple, a bride in a full wedding dress and a groom in top hat and tails who were intent on stopping at a small church along the route, getting married and then finishing the race as man and wife.

Once at the start, a throng of over 40,000 runners stood in the shivering cold awaiting the starting gun, which appeared to be a large artillery piece left over from World War II. Bonnie went off to visit Greenwich's famous meridian, where she stood—one foot in the western hemisphere and the other in the eastern hemisphere—while John took her photograph.

Back at the race, the gun went off, but nothing happened. There was such a large crowd of runners that no one in the crush of bodies could move for about five minutes, but eventually they were off. David's intention was to maintain a speed of seven-and-one-half miles per hour, or eight-minute miles, but the slow start and crowded conditions made it impossible.

Eventually everyone started moving at just a shuffle and after five or ten minutes he was able to lengthen his stride and pick up the pace, being careful not to tread on another runner's heels.

The weather conditions were cloudy and cool, just perfect for running, and the sights along the way were magnificent. He passed the famous *Cutty Sark* tea clipper with a military band on board, ran over Tower Bridge and alongside the Tower of London where the organizers had thoughtfully laid rubber matting over the cobblestones.

He passed numerous pubs that were handing out orange quarters to the runners and there were thousands of cheering spectators lining the route in something approaching a carnival atmosphere.

At the halfway mark, he was well into a comfortable running pace, had broken into a light sweat and was grateful for the many water stations where small bottles of cool water were handed to the runners as they came past.

At about the 22-mile point, David began to tire and feared that he might be hitting the runner's dreaded 'wall'. Another runner came alongside him and urged him to keep going and he would get through it. She appeared considerably older than David, said she had run the London marathon 22 times and then took off leaving him in her dust.

He managed to run through his fatigue and soon Buckingham Palace came into view and as he drew closer David could have sworn, he could see the queen waving to him. Then he was past, the finish was in sight and as he crossed the line someone hung a finishers medal around his neck. He had completed the run in three hours and 40 minutes, averaging just under 8.4 minutes per mile.

He spent five minutes resting under a tree before looking for the rest of his party. Once he had located them, John took his photograph and what sorry sight he was. Then they were off to see David's niece, John's daughter, who had just had a baby, before taking the long drive back to Hampshire. The following day, David mailed a postcard to his doctor proudly announcing that what she had called his 'pipe dream' had become a reality.

Returning to Vancouver, it was decided that as David was retiring at year-end, Bonnie would terminate her employment and they would definitely move to Florida where Bonnie could look after her mother and David could launch into a new career as an artist.

To do this, David had to travel to the U.S. Embassy in Ottawa and apply for a green card, which would allow him to reside and work in the United States. He was told that this would take some time, as background checks had to be made and fingerprints taken, but the process had started and once again he was on the move.

***

On the art scene, David decided that his new career upon arriving in Florida would be as a watercolor artist, quite a deviation from the oil painting that he had been using. To test the waters, he decided to hold an exhibition of his work in Vancouver.

An intense period of painting followed during which time he produced a number of pieces, some oil, some water color and some charcoal. The subjects were mostly seascapes and maritime scenes, with a couple of nude sketches thrown in to add a little spice to the collection.

The exhibit was set up in the common area of a downtown shopping mall with a cheese and wine opening before the week-long exhibition. The artwork was well received with several pieces sold and David's career as a starving artist was born! Limited edition prints were made of some of the work and one was even purchased by the federal government.

To the best of his knowledge, it still hangs in the Vancouver offices of the Canadian Department of Oceans and Fisheries.

By this time, David's daughter Karen had graduated from high school and was working in a large sporting goods store in West Vancouver. She had attended a French immersion school, was bilingual in French and English and was eager to find work that would enable her to travel abroad.

David put her in touch with an agency that recruited staff for the cruise ship industry and at the age of nineteen, she began a life at sea on a cruise ship sailing out of New Orleans.

David well remembers waving goodbye to her at the Vancouver airport with some trepidation as she embarked on her own life of thrills and adventure.

As the year-end approached, David received his green card to live and work in the United States. Most of their household effects were divided among the children, and they sold Bonnie's Toyota and rented a U-Haul truck that would take the remainder of their belongings to Florida.

Their fifth wedding anniversary, 31 December 1999, their final night living in Canada, was spent sleeping on the floor of their house and in the early morning of the beginning of the new millennium, they set off for the U.S. border.

147

Chapter Fifteen

The first destination on their journey south was to visit David's old Guardforce business partner Nick, who had emigrated from South Africa to the U.S. several years previously and now lived in La Jolla, near San Diego.

Interestingly, on their drive down to San Diego along the coast road, they encountered a large herd of elephant seals in northern California. There were forty or fifty of them just casually lounging on the beach while several onlookers just strolled among them.

When they arrived at Nick's house the poor chap was horrified to see the Birds' ratty old U-Haul truck pull into the front of his house, a magnificent, multimillion-dollar home set in a beautifully manicured garden on the very top of Black Gold Road.

Once introductions and handshakes were dealt with, their hosts' first priority was to move the U-Haul truck around to the back of the house where no one could see it, especially the neighbors, whose Rolls Royce was parked in their forecourt.

A pleasant couple of days were spent in La Jolla and then they were off to Las Vegas, where David attended a three-day picture framing convention. Framing was the most expensive aspect of art and an artist's nightmare, so David invested several thousand dollars in framing equipment so that he could frame his own paintings.

Although David had visited Las Vegas once before, he was no more impressed with it this time around. They met up with some friends and saw a couple of shows, none of which were particularly good, but they didn't go to any casinos since neither of them were gamblers.

From Las Vegas, they drove through several states along Interstate 10, reaching Port Orange 10 days after leaving Vancouver. Significant points of interest along the way were getting a flat tire on a deserted patch of the interstate in Texas, which took several hours to get repaired and picking up daughter Karen who had been shipwrecked near Jamaica and was stranded in Mobile, Alabama.

The vessel had apparently caught fire and all the passengers were taken ashore and flown home. The ship then limped back to Alabama for repairs.

The three of them arrived in Port Orange on 10 January. Bonnie's mother was surprised and delighted to find that she had three new arrivals rather than the two she had expected and was anxious to hear all their news. They promptly unloaded the truck and turned it in to an amazed U-Haul agency in Port Orange when they saw the mileage.

Once David and Bonnie were settled in, Karen was packed off back to her ship in Mobile via a Greyhound bus. David's framing workshop was set up in one of the four garages and he quickly found and joined the Daytona Beach Art League.

He was also delighted to discover that nearby Daytona Beach had a rowing club, which he promptly joined. The club was a sculling club and David, recalling his miserable attempt at sculling on the river Thames, was grateful for the ministrations of an elderly founder of the club, who was still a very competent sculler and taught him to become at least an upright one.

Work began on a series of paintings, mostly watercolors, that had a nautical flavor with many graceful tall ships. By early April, David was ready for his first art show and a selection of paintings were framed and put on sale at a local show in Ponce Inlet with the result that three were sold and several positive compliments received.

David continued with his running, usually consisting of six miles crossing the Intracoastal Waterway and along the beach and back, which he performed three days a week. Bonnie bought a speedometer-equipped bicycle and accompanied him on his runs, sharply criticizing him if his speed dropped below 7 m.p.h.

Their second art show was in Cocoa Beach and it was there that David met a man who was to become a very good friend. They met at the men's toilet!

The Cocoa Beach art show had over 100 artists in attendance but only one men's toilet—kindly made available to the participating artists by the town's fire department. The show was a two-day affair and the toilet, a one-seater, was in constant use. On one occasion when David went there, the door was closed and a solitary gentleman was waiting his turn. They each gave the other a cursory nod and waited…and waited.

Eventually, the patient gentleman turned to David and said that he had been waiting for several minutes. He spoke with an English accent, which David commented on and asked which part of England he came from.

The surprising reply was 'Shepherd's Bush'. "So am I," said David.

As the conversation developed, it turned out that they were both born at London's Queen Charlotte's hospital and both now lived on Riverside Drive in Port Orange!

After chatting for several more minutes, there was still no sign of the toilet occupant, so David tried the door. It was not locked and there was no one inside! If it were not for the fellow Londoner's inept testing of the door handle, they would never have struck up a conversation and probably would have never met.

His newfound friend Ken, took David to meet his wife Judy, who was the artist in the family. Ken and Judy were then introduced to Bonnie and a great friendship developed between the two couples. Dinner and cards every Saturday night and a lady cyclist to accompany Bonnie on David's thrice-weekly runs.

Painting, picture framing, running and rowing occupied much of David's time and he was attending between twelve and sixteen art shows per year. Sales were pretty consistent with the sale of original works supplemented by gift cards and prints in assorted sizes.

One disconcerting fact that David could not ignore since arriving in the United States was the number of people who were overweight, fat or obese. No matter where he looked, a large percentage of the population was of gigantic proportions and seemingly oblivious of the fact.

Even the television programs seemed to deal with it as though it were normal, but he couldn't equate this phenomenon with the athletic lifestyle that the U.S. projects.

In 2001, David was asked to manage the Daytona Beach rowing club, named the Halifax Rowing Association because of its location on the Halifax River, which is a section of the Intracoastal Waterway. For a small remuneration, he accepted the position on the condition that sweep rowing would be added to the sculling program that was already well established.

The clubhouse was shared with Embry Riddle Aeronautical University's rowing club, which had several eight shells, two of which they were not using and which they generously loaned to Halifax to get the rowing program started.

Through a variety of creative methods, David recruited many men and women to the rowing program and as he became more confident in his role as coach, so residents living along the Halifax River became accustomed to being woken up to the sound of his exhortations over a bullhorn, encouraging his crews to greater effort.

Through a series of fundraising efforts, including a great deal of help from the Port Orange YMCA, and with a greatly increased club membership, the two eights on loan from Embry Riddle bit the dust and several eight seat and four seat shells were purchased.

The 'masters' program grew from strength to strength and a high school program was developed. The HRA members attended several regattas annually and became a force to be reckoned with on the Florida rowing circuit.

A visit to the boathouse today demonstrates the prowess of Halifax as a successful rowing club. Hundreds of medals still hang from the rafters and those are just a fraction of the ones won by Halifax.

David recalls with bitterness the morning of Wednesday, 11 September 2001. He had just finished straightening up the boathouse after an early morning row and was about to lock up when an elderly member of the club turned up to use one of the rowing machines.

He asked David, "Have you heard this morning's news?" and receiving a negative reply told him of an airplane that had crashed into a skyscraper in the middle of New York City.

He knew no more than that, but when David returned home, the full horror of that awful day became apparent.

Of course, for days, weeks and months, talking heads on the TV pontificated on their opinions and judgments. David couldn't understand the U.S. government's weak response. Retaliating against Afghanistan was understandable, but he felt that if Islam, as a whole, could rejoice and celebrate this attack, then Islam, in its entirety, should be blamed and punished.

Innocent and blameless people would undoubtedly suffer, but innocent and blameless people suffered during the Second World War when Japanese, German, British and American forces bombed cities indiscriminately. It's called collateral damage.

David is the first to acknowledge that it's easy to become an armchair critic after the fact and is well aware that there were many behind-the-scene happenings that the public was not made aware of. Just like mushrooms, they stay in the dark and are fed shit.

Sadly, David's mother died in 2003 at the age of 96. When David heard that the end was near, he flew over to England and visited her in hospital. She was in a comatose state much of the time, but when he last visited her before flying home, he was by her bedside while his brother and sister waited outside.

Speaking to her softly but presuming that she heard nothing, he was amazed when she stirred, opened her eyes and said, quite clearly, "David, you're a good guy," and then fell asleep.

It still seems hard to believe. His mother was unlikely to use the word 'guy'.

'Bloke' perhaps or even 'man', but 'guy'?

Nevertheless, she said it, he heard it, and those words, possibly the last words she ever uttered, will stay with him for the rest of his life.

In early 2005, Bonnie's mother also died and Bonnie inherited the house. David stayed continually busy with his art shows and his work began to change from nautical themes toward surrealism, which seemed to have a greater appeal.

He was also heavily committed to the rowing club and had managed to persuade Bonnie to become a member. Surprisingly, she took to rowing like a duck to water and was especially valuable, being petite and agile, as their number one coxswain.

***

On an unforgettable trip later that year, they joined two other couples and rented a catamaran for ten days in the British Virgin Islands. They flew first into Puerto Rico and from there on to the island of Tortola. One of the men traveling with them had his captain's license, and with plenty of crew it was easy sailing—the weather was gorgeous and the islands spectacular.

It is believed that the British Virgin Islands have been inhabited since 1500 BC, but history shows that the first documented inhabitants were the Arawaks, who arrived around 100 BC. The more aggressive Caribs displaced the South American Arawaks during the fifteenth century, not long before Christopher Columbus spotted the islands in 1493.

David, Bonnie and friends visited the four large islands of Tortola, Anegada, Virgin Gorda and Jost Van Dyke and were amazed at how quiet and secluded they were. They were surprised to find the very crude and ancient Callwood Rum Distillery on Tortola.

Apparently, the Callwood family took over the distillery in the eighteenth century and has been producing rum for over 200 years. Probably a hangover from some pirate crew or others desperate for some grog.

One of the highlights of their trip was meeting up with a fellow sailor who was sailing the islands with his two sons. The father was captain of one of the U.S. Navy's aircraft carriers, which made for some very interesting conversations. However, what impressed David the most was that they were returning home the following day and as a parting gift, the sailor and his sons gave them six dozen cans of Heineken that they had no further use for. Cheers!

Running had become a way of life for David and he made many friends and acquaintances on the running circuit. He also became convinced that the exercise that he gained from rowing and running was, to a very large degree, offsetting the detrimental effects that diabetes was having on his body. He had been insulin dependent since 1999 but did not find the five times-a-day injections particularly onerous.

***

David was very anxious to show Bonnie Africa, particularly South Africa, which was still reasonably safe and well governed, so in 2006, they took an extended holiday to South Africa via a few days with David's sister in Hampshire. They flew into Johannesburg, where they were met by David's old friends from Salisbury and Coffee Bay, John and Jean.

By this time, South Africa had dispensed with white rule and its apartheid policy. Crime had become a serious problem and virtually every house was surrounded by huge security walls or fencing, with each becoming something of an impregnable fortress.

Fortunately, Nelson Mandela had recognized the errors of his brethren further north and encouraged most of the Europeans to remain in South Africa rather than drive them out. As a result, the infrastructure and economy remained basically sound.

While in Johannesburg, they were able to go down into one of the gold mines on the reef, see how the gold was mined and later smelted and turned into a bar of gold. Bonnie was permitted to hold one once it had cooled down, but unfortunately it wouldn't fit in her handbag!

Having rented a car in Johannesburg, they drove 300 miles east to enter the magnificent Kruger National Park. They stayed in the park for a week, living in a small thatched rondavel, driving out every morning and evening to search for game and seeing an abundance of elephant, buffalo, crocodile, zebra and kudu.

The list could go on and on, but one spectacular sighting was when three male cheetahs stepped out right in front of their car. Bonnie, a camera buff, took a multitude of photographs that would always serve as a reminder of her first trip to Africa.

Just outside the park, they visited the privately run Moholoholo Wildlife Rehabilitation Center and the Hoedspruit Cheetah Project, where Bonnie got to pet and stroke an adult cheetah. There was also a baby hippopotamus named Humphrey, who followed their tour guide around religiously, gumming his leg the whole time, for he had not yet developed teeth.

Humphrey had apparently been deserted by his mother and would stay at the rehabilitation center until he could be reintroduced into the wild. Who knows?...He looked like he was enjoying himself so much that perhaps he never left.

While staying at these two centers, they also toured in an open land cruiser, accompanied by a rifle toting game warden, viewing uncaged lions, leopards, rhinos, zebras and crocodiles and also some honey badgers and vultures in separate compounds.

From Kruger National Park, they drove south into Swaziland (now Eswatini), a landlocked country bordered by Mozambique and South Africa. It is one of the smallest countries in Africa, but its climate ranges from the cool and mountainous Highveld to the hot and dry Lowveld. After the Boer War, Swaziland became a British territory in 1903 until gaining full independence in 1968.

While in Swaziland, they spent two nights at the Mlilwane Wildlife Sanctuary in a small but comfortable cabin. Not much game was in evidence, but a very tame kudu followed them around the camp, perhaps hoping for a free meal or two.

From Swaziland, they drove south into Natal Province in South Africa and through the Valley of a Thousand Hills. The drive was absolutely awesome and they certainly appreciated the beauty of nature all around them.

This area is home to the Zulu people and is frequently referred to as Zululand, where the famous king Shaka of the Zulus reigned from 1816 until 1828. Shaka ordered far-reaching reforms and reorganized the military into a formidable force.

Their next stop was in Durban, where David had lived for several years and where he first established the Guardforce security company. They visited David's old friends Bobbi and Pete, whom he had known since living next door to them at Park Vista in Umtali in 1969 and they arranged marvelous ocean front accommodation for them at the nearby resort town of Umhlanga Rocks, which, although very small, has a most magnificent coastline, viewpoints and beaches.

***

Unfortunately, Mr. B, at the age of 92, died just before David and Bonnie arrived in South Africa. To the best of David's knowledge, Mr. B's collection of gold coins, diamonds, his South African financial assets and other personal belongings either reverted to the state or were purloined by the assisted living facility where he was living.

Even his will never came to light, primarily due to his accountant or lawyer having been murdered just one week before his own death. Fortunately, his grandson Keith managed to salvage finances invested in the British Channel Islands, which went to Mr. B's two daughters.

No one was with him at the end of his incredible life and none of his family were present when he was put to rest. Neither of Mr. B's daughters were close to him, geographically or emotionally, although Joyce did speak with him by telephone quite regularly.

Durban is a long way from Vancouver and a journey of that nature could be quite daunting for many single women. David presumed that all that needed to be said between Joyce and her father was said and he chose to remain silent.

Mr. B was probably cremated and his ashes thrown to the four winds. David, who could have helped to some degree though no longer related, would almost certainly have been viewed as acting in self-interest and therefore decided not to get involved.

Mr. B did not suffer fools gladly, wasn't afraid to speak his mind and perhaps lacked some social skills, but David salutes one of the finest men it was ever his good fortune to meet.

***

While spending a few days in Durban, together with Bobbi and Pete, they visited some of David's old haunts along the Natal south coast. Seaside towns such as Amanzimtoti and especially Margate where he and his family spent several holidays while living in Rhodesia. He was just enjoying reliving some old memories. They also had a memorable visit to a Zulu village in the Valley of a Thousand Hills.

While watching some tribal dancing, David recalled an earlier visit some 20 years previously when nubile maidens clad only in brief skirts allowed their breasts to swing freely. On this occasion, the dancers were not so nubile and were fully clothed, albeit in traditional clothing. David blames the missionaries!

Having dropped off their rental car, Bobbi and Pete drove them to the Durban airport, where they took a flight south to East London.

While sitting at the airport waiting for their flight, Pete pointed out the new livery on all the South African Airways aircraft, commenting on the red, green and black design on the tail.

"The black represents the people; the red represents the blood that was shed in gaining freedom; and the green represents the fertility of the land."

He then sarcastically added that the thin white line surrounding the design was what was holding the whole thing together!

East London is a city on the southeast coast of South Africa, largely situated between the Buffalo River and the Nahoon River and is home to South Africa's only river port. In the early to mid-19th century, during the frontier wars between the British settlers and the local Xhosa inhabitants, this port was used as a supply port to service the military headquarters at nearby King William's Town about 30 miles away.

From East London, they drove to Port Elizabeth, frequently referred to simply as P.E. or The Windy City, which is situated on Algoa Bay. It is at the northern end of The Garden Route and David was looking forward to introducing Bonnie to this fantastic portion of their journey.

If the whole world is indeed a garden, as Frances Hodgson Burnett once wrote, then the Garden Route of South Africa was cultivated by a maverick horticulturist. Covering 200 miles of coastline and extending far inwards, it comprises a variety of landscapes that merge into a dramatic meeting of mountains, gorges, forests and ocean that are dotted along the way by several quaint towns and beach cities.

The first spot they reached was Mossel Bay, which marks the spot where the very first Europeans set foot in South Africa. This prestigious honor was bestowed upon the Portuguese explorer Bartolomeu Dias in 1488.

The cave network below Pinnacle Point once contained some of the earliest artifacts of modern man. They are believed to be about 164,000 years old and these days a visit to Mossel Bay would not be complete without visiting the caves and museum.

David regrets that he had failed to take this opportunity previously, although he had driven through Mossel Bay several times while living in Rhodesia and South Africa.

Their next stop was in the town of George, one of South Africa's oldest towns and a historic timber hub nestled in the Outeniqua Mountains. David enjoyed showing Bonnie some of the glorious scenic drives in the area and the multitude of antique shops, art galleries and craft stalls.

Traveling inland, they entered the sparse Klein Karoo desert and the town of Oudtshoorn, an area known as home to the largest ostrich population in the world. Traditionally, the ostriches were bred for their feathers, which before World War I, were the country's fourth largest export and worth almost their weight in diamonds! Today, they are bred primarily for their very healthy meat.

Bonnie got to ride an ostrich and had a furry neck rub from two very tame ostriches. David was limited to feeding an ostrich with a pellet held between his lips and watching ostrich jockeys roar around a dirt racetrack.

From Outshoorn, they returned to the coast and their next stop was at the small town of Knysna, which must be one of the most beautiful spots in all of Africa. The Knysna River feeds a warm water estuary and passes through two prominent headlands—The Knysna Heads—creating a treacherous stretch of water as it flows into the Indian Ocean.

From Knysna, continuing their journey south, they entered the Tsisikamma National Park, which is a protected area covering 50 miles of coastline known for its indigenous forests. At the southern end, the Storms River flows into the ocean and nearby is the Bloukrans Bridge, which offers the highest bridge bungee jump in the world. It goes without saying that neither David nor Bonnie tried it.

They did, however, take the zipline, the first of its kind in Africa. They were zip-lining from one platform to another along a steel cable suspended up to 100 feet above the forest and, coincidentally, met up with a couple from Bielefeld, Germany, where David's brother John was stationed while serving in the R.E.M.E. in the mid-1950s. The zip line was fast, the experience unforgettable and the views beyond description.

The next stop along the Garden Route was the town of Plettenberg Bay, where David spent his first honeymoon back in 1966 at Mr. and Mrs. B's holiday apartment. He found that it hadn't changed much. The beaches were as beautiful as ever, dominated by the long, rocky peninsula known as Robberg.

Not wanting to linger over times past, David suggested that they leave the Garden Route and travel west to the small town of Villiersdorp, where they spent a few days with two of David's old Rhodesian friends who were now retired. They enjoyed a few relaxing days with them, visiting several wineries in and around the Stellenbosch area.

It was a special treat when they drove to Boulders Beach, famous for its large colony of African penguins, formerly known as 'jackass' penguins. They were allowed to walk the beach alongside the penguins and were amused at their behavior and antics.

They also visited the lighthouse at the tip of the Cape of Good Hope—a good climb, but they accessed it part of the way by means of a very steep funicular.

From Cape Town, they flew home again via England at the conclusion of an absolutely unforgettable holiday.

Chapter Sixteen

Around this time, the rowing club was involved in entering crews in several had races. A head race, or head of the river race to give it its proper title, is usually about three miles long and one memorable event was held in Miami.

David was in the men's eight and they were very impressed to find that one of the opposing crews was the Australian national men's eight, which had come over to compete in an international regatta that would take place in the United States later that same month.

The Halifax crew were one of the first boats to start, with the usual ten-second gap between each crew being the norm. The Australian crew, being the obvious favorites, were the last to leave.

David's crew were well down the course before the Australians came into sight far, far behind them. Halifax put the pedal to the metal, hoping to hold off the Australians for as long as possible, but those Aussies came down the river like a freight train, flying past the Halifax boat as if it were hardly moving. A thoroughly humiliating experience.

Halifax had also entered several crews in a large head race that is held annually on the Chattahoochee River in Chattanooga, Tennessee, a regatta generally known as 'The Hootch'. Hundreds of crews took part during the two-day event and competition was fierce.

David's crew of four men, with Bonnie as coxswain, was considered an extreme outsider, as all four of them were in their late sixties and were sarcastically known as the fossil four!

The course was over three miles and anything under 20 minutes was considered a good finishing time. Because of their age, they were given a small handicap advantage of about two minutes, but with 22 boats in the fossil four's event, many being college crews, and being a timed event, each crew left the start separately and the fossil four's chances of finishing anywhere but last were minimal.

They got off to a fine start, maintained a higher rating than usual and caught a rhythm that just seemed to click. Bonnie steered a magnificent course down the winding Chattahoochee and they were well pleased with themselves though thoroughly exhausted when they crossed the finishing line in well under 20 minutes. When they later discovered that they had earned the bronze medal for gaining third place, they were ecstatic.

Two years later, David and the fossil four, by then really decrepit, earned another bronze medal at the Hooch' when forming half of the Halifax men's eight at the same event.

***

Visits to British Columbia were taken every two or three years. Sean, Keith and Karen were busy with their own lives and in time married and produced a total of five grandchildren. Trips up to Smithers in northern British Columbia involved a two-day drive from Vancouver and resulted in sightings of moose, bear and on one occasion a herd of over 20 wild horses led by a magnificent stallion.

One trip to visit Keith resulted in a one-day drive to Hyder, Alaska. Hyder is accessible only by road from the town of Stewart in British Columbia and has a population of less than 100 people. Amazingly, they saw several grizzly bears standing in the river snatching up huge salmon as they struggled upstream to spawn. After taking just one big bite, they would toss the salmon aside to grab another tasty morsel.

Anyone visiting Hyder might find it challenging to get Hyderised. One of the two pubs in this small town mixes an alcoholic concoction to which is added an old prospector's big toe, kept for this purpose in a jar of formaldehyde. The concoction is then swigged back, the toe returned to its jar and the imbiber welcomed to this very elite club. David is not a member but understands that both Karen and Keith couldn't resist the challenge!

On another trip to visit Keith, who was now married with two small children, David decided that on the route from Vancouver to Smithers they would stop at the old gold-mining town of Barkerville. This was the main town of the Cariboo Gold Rush and is preserved as a historic town.

It was named after Billy Barker, who came from England and was among the first to strike gold in 1861. This, the richest and most famous claim in the area, would eventually yield over 37,000 ounces of gold.

Barkerville grew rapidly as thousands of fortune seekers arrived—some on foot with merely a backpack, others in a pack train until a road was built enabling huge freight wagons to transport men, women and children. The town grew with a church, a hotel, a theater, a brothel, plenty of saloons and many commercial establishments being established and a boom town was born.

Many Chinese immigrants also arrived in Barkerville, mostly as laborer's but some as merchants, and they were to play a large part in the development of the town.

In 1868, Barkerville was destroyed by a fire that quickly spread through the wooden buildings, but the town was quickly rebuilt with a widened street, better boardwalks and even a small school for its dozen or so children. The population, however, began to decline as gold became more and more scarce until what was left in the mid- to late 1930s was a very small village.

In 1959, the Barkerville Historic Park was established by BC Parks. Buildings were restored and much later, as tourism increased, the small theater performed period vaudeville productions; some shops were opened and the employees were required to wear costumes appropriate to the 1860s.

The Barkerville Hotel was reopened and although it had only six bedrooms, David and Bonnie acquired one and spent the night in their quaint and tiny wooden hotel and enjoying a communal breakfast with fellow guests from all over Canada and the United States.

***

During the intervening years between when David arrived in the United States at the age of 55 and reaching the legitimate retirement age of 65, his two sons, Keith and Sean, had each gained a wife and each had two young sons. These boys, aged somewhere between six and nine, were somewhat familiar with Grandad and Grandma Bonnie, as their parents brought them to Florida or David and Bonnie would fly up to British Columbia quite frequently.

David decided he would have to do something special for them the next time they came to Florida, so he devised a plan. Their house was right on the banks of the Intracoastal Waterway, but not on the main channel.

There was a string of totally deserted islands several miles long that stretched along the west side of the channel and was maintained as a bird sanctuary by the Audubon Society. Their house looked out over the calm waters of the lagoon toward these islands, which were no more than a half mile distant and which sheltered the main channel from view.

David had a small rowing dingy that, in a pinch, could hold four individuals and gave him access to the islands from his small dock at the water's edge.

With plenty of advance warning of the arrival of Keith's family, he set about making two small wooden chests, complete with brass hinges and handles and well varnished. He and Bonnie then set about finding suitable pirate treasures to fill the chests and succeeded in locating many of these rare and valuable treasures at Walt Disney World in Orlando.

The treasure chests were filled with glass beads that represented diamonds, rubies and emeralds, a telescope, an eye patch and a headscarf, plus a few other bits and pieces. David, armed with a shovel, rowed across to one of the islands in his small dinghy.

Determining two likely spots, he set about burying the two chests and subtly marked the spots with a couple of logs that he found lying about and the shell of a large horseshoe crab that had conveniently died nearby.

Now came the tricky part. He found two sheets of parchment-like paper, soaked them in cold tea and when they were dry tore and burned the edges to give the impression that they were very old.

He then composed two poems, one on each parchment, supposedly reflecting an old pirate's directions to find the buried booty. Using his best attempts at calligraphy with India ink, David wrote the following:

Black Dog's Treasure

The pathway east from Sunshine Beach
Leads to a junction at two hundred feet
Of fig and fir trees from which you see
A tall free-standing lone palm tree
Turn south-east and you will see
Yet another lone palm tree
Three paces beyond lies a cross of logs
Beneath which lies the treasure of Black Dog

<u>*Serpent's Breath Treasure*</u>

From Sunshine Beach take path at left
Find fig and fir trees at eighty steps
Look for lone palm tree to the east
Five and twenty steps at least
Serpent's Breath treasure lies beneath the sand
Just five steps south from where a palm tree stands
The spot is covered by the shell
Of a giant horseshoe crab—look well

Following the pirate's directions, David sketched a map showing the fig, fir and palm trees with an 'X' marking the spot on each of the parchments.

The next week Keith, his wife and their two boys aged seven and eight arrived and after a day or two David took the boys aside and told them a pack of lies.

He described how an old man had given him two old scrolls which were supposed to reveal the whereabouts of some hidden treasure. He told them that he thought it was a load of old rubbish, but the boys begged and pestered to be shown the scrolls, which he eventually and very reluctantly did.

After scrutinizing them at some length, they took them to their parents who, incidentally, had not been privy to the deception but obviously saw that Grandad's devious hand was at play.

David admitted to the boys that he did know of a Sunshine Beach on one of the islands, a name he had made up, for it was no more than a muddy patch where he had previously landed his rowboat.

The following day with David at the oars, son Keith and the two boys boarded the dinghy, taking with them some shovels and a picnic lunch. Their mother and grandma Bonnie joined them in two borrowed kayaks.

Upon arriving at Sunshine Beach, the boats were dragged ashore and the boys went running off with their parchments, totally clueless as to where they were going.

Eventually, Mom and Dad restored order and after studying the maps themselves and with a bit of nudging by David, both the crossed logs and the horseshoe crab shell were discovered.

Digging began in earnest and sure enough, first one and then the other, discovered the two chests. When they were opened and the contents revealed, the two boys were ecstatic with glee. Eye patches were adorned, telescopes opened and treasures studied with great interest. For the remainder of their stay, those two boys were never without their headscarves, eye patches and telescopes and David was well pleased with his efforts.

To this day, both boys still have those old wooden treasure chests and the maps that led to them. Hopefully, when they have children of their own, they will tell the story of the Black Dog and Serpent's Breath treasures.

The following year, Sean's family arrived for a two-week vacation and David repeated the performance for his two sons then aged eight and six. This time the pirates were Hateful Henry and Left Hand Luke and their directions to the treasure were as follows:

The Treasure of Hateful Henry

From Sunset Beach walk ninety paces
Pass between a spruce and fig
Turn right, bear left and seek ye
The witches fire circle
Beyond pass through two palms before you
And you'll spy a twin palm tree
Beneath a square of palm frond pieces
Hateful Henry's treasure may be

The Treasure of Left Hand Luke

From Sunrise Beach on Pirate Island
Seek a stunted lone palm tree
Take thirty paces westwards
Where another two you'll see
A small cross lie between them
Sunk into the island sand
Beneath this cross there lies my treasure
And perhaps my lost right hand

Several people learned of David's pirate adventures and tried to convince him that he might have hit upon an idea with considerable potential. He resisted any attempts to persuade him thus and has never visited the pirate island again.

When his daughter Karen married and had a little boy some ten years later, David realized that he had one more duty to perform and with his latest grandson now turned six, he had better get started. At the time of this writing, he is still contemplating his options.

Chapter Seventeen

David's wanderlust was still not satisfied and at the age of 65 and still in good health, he decided that they should see more of the world. Therefore, in 2009, after a brief visit to England, David and Bonnie flew to Bergerac in the Dordogne area of France, rented a car and drove to the small town of Martell where David's cousin and her husband lived.

They took them to several nearby points of interest, the most fascinating being Rocamadour. Set in a gorge above a tributary of the river Dordogne, it is famous for its historical monuments and the sanctuary of the Blessed Virgin Mary.

Rocamadour was built on a rock wall where the mummified body of an old hermit was discovered. The site is incredible as it clings to the rock wall, and, in some cases, the buildings are partly excavated into the rock face. A huge church nearby was hewn out of and dug into the rock over a thousand years ago.

The multitude of steps cut into the rock leading up to the church are worn thin by the millions of worshippers who were forced to crawl up and down them rather than walk. Hard to figure—yes?

From Martell, they drove east to the foothills of the French Alps, where one of David's old police friends, Roger and his wife Sue, owned a small hotel, the Auberge Camelia, in the tiny town of Aviernoz. They stayed a few days and visited the beautiful town of Annecy, which lies on the northern tip of Lake Annecy, just 20 miles from Geneva, Switzerland.

David visited their rowing club and was impressed by the boathouse and the range of rowing shells and sculls. The coach was busy instructing a group of beginner scullers, setting them afloat on broad, stable, flat-bottomed craft rather than putting them directly into the long, thin and unstable single-scull, which was David's introduction to sculling.

Arrangements had been made for a few ex-BSAP friends to visit from England and, along with several expatriates from England now living in France, made a delightful evening of eating, drinking and making merry.

Roger was pals with a Frenchman who owned an isolated restaurant high in the mountains. Autumn was approaching, the weather was getting chilly and the friend's restaurant was closed for the season. However, with a bit of arm twisting, he agreed to provide dinner for their small group and they were conveyed to the restaurant in his rather battered old mini-bus.

The food was great, the atmosphere terrific and the company beyond compare, but to top it all, David found a plaque outside the restaurant door proclaiming that this was the spot where the first allied parachute drop to French resistance forces had been made during World War II.

From Aviernoz, David and Bonnie drove up into the Alps and through the Mont Blanc tunnel into Italy. The tunnel, completed in 1962, was built in a joint venture between France and Italy. What a difference, David found, between entering the tunnel in France and exiting it in Italy.

Whereas the French gardens were well maintained and their window boxes full of colorful blooms, Italy by comparison was full of mad drivers and neglected houses, but where even the shoeshine boys wore Armani suits.

They visited Florence, which, due to its artistic and architectural heritage, was ranked by Forbes one year later as the most beautiful city in the world. They visited the museum containing Michelangelo's famous statue of David and our David was amused to see that sitting on a long wooden bench behind the statue were seven or eight elderly ladies gazing up at his magnificent butt.

As someone of mediocre artistic talent, David had to admit that the statue was absolutely brilliant, although he had to agree with the many critics who have suggested that David's right hand is disproportionately larger than the rest of him.

Then it was on to Pisa to see the famous leaning tower. It was indeed leaning and no one was allowed to enter, but there were many other intriguing religious buildings and artifacts in the well-maintained enclosure to provide for an entertaining outing.

The city of Pisa straddles the Arno River just before it empties into the Ligurian Sea. David was delighted to see some rowing activity on the river and was tempted to find the club and go for a row, but having no kit and not sure where to start looking, he let it pass.

He will admit that he saw only a very small part of Italy and that from what he has heard it is a beautiful country, but from the small part that he did see he was not impressed.

From Pisa, they drove back into France, returned to the Auberge Camelia for a final visit with Roger before driving on to Geneva in Switzerland for the flight home.

***

Just over two years later, a visit to Australia was on the agenda and hating winter, even in balmy Florida, David and Bonnie flew into sunny Sydney. Instead of driving, they chose to use the train system on this trip and began their Australian visit by exploring Sydney. They found it to be a huge, bustling and vibrant city with a surprisingly large Chinese population.

George Street led from their hotel all the way down to Sydney Harbor, where a large ferry terminal at the shoreline provided water transport to a multitude of destinations. An aborigine playing a digeridoo gave a traditional flavor to the experience while they waited for a ferry to one of the islands containing the world-famous Taronga Zoo. The zoo was exceptional and of particular interest were the koalas and the Tasmanian devils.

While in Sydney, they also visited the landmark Sydney Opera House and the Sydney Harbor Bridge.

From Sydney, they traveled by train to Melbourne, where they were met by Kiwi and his wife, who had come over especially from New Zealand to meet them. Since they were staying with their daughter, who lived in Melbourne, they were killing two birds with one stone.

Kiwi had access to a car for the week that they were in Melbourne, so they were able to visit several points of interest and even took in a day at the Australian Open tennis championship to see Venus Williams, Andy Roddick and Justine Henning in action. They all won!

An interesting building that caught David's attention was the Flinders Street Railway Station. This historic railway station, on the corner of Flinders and Swanston streets, is in the central business district of Melbourne, and although it opened back in 1854, it still serves the entire metropolitan rail network.

Two large parks dominate the city, the first being Queen Victoria Gardens, which comprises 12 acres in the center of Melbourne. Upon her death in 1901, it was thought appropriate to install an enduring monument to her reign and a statue was commissioned showing the queen in ceremonial gowns as she cast her regal gaze across the ornamental lakes, sweeping lawns and rose gardens.

The second is Alexandra Gardens, another twelve-acre park on the opposite side of the Yarra River. What fascinated David the most was that the Yarra River, which meanders directly through the gardens, had six or seven rowing clubs along its banks and he enjoyed watching several crews at practice on more than one occasion. He also enjoyed having a lengthy conversation with one of the club's coaches.

Having spent a week in the company of Kiwi and his family, David and Bonnie took a train to Adelaide where after a brief stay, they boarded The Ghan for an almost 2,000-mile journey north across Australia to Darwin. The Ghan is a train named after the Afghan cameleers who from the 1860s until the early 20th century helped explore and build infrastructures in the outback.

Once The Ghan began rolling, there was no longer a need for the camels, so they were let loose to roam the vast deserts of central Australia. Today, there are approximately 300,000 wild camels in the Australian hinterland.

The Ghan only makes the journey once a week in each direction, with only one stop at a small town called Alice Springs. David, an avid reader, had been enthralled years earlier by Neville Shute's book *A Town Like Alice* and thought it would be a good idea to stop there for a week.

The journey from Adelaide to Alice Springs took around 24 hours and was rather uncomfortable, as David had chosen to book seats rather than a sleeper cabin. However, they arrived in mid-afternoon, collected their luggage and followed the few passengers that were disembarking onto the forecourt.

Taxi cabs took those few passengers away, someone locked up the station and departed. David and Bonnie were left standing outside with no one in sight—no taxi and no telephone.

After waiting for about 30 minutes while expecting a taxi to appear, David left Bonnie with the luggage and began the long, dusty walk in the blazing heat to the distant town of Alice. The walk took about 30 minutes, a taxi was located and Bonnie was collected. Then on to their hotel, booked long in advance, called The Jolly Swagman.

The young woman at the reception desk was surprisingly a South African with a warm welcome. After getting settled in their room, David fancied a cup of tea and asked if they had a teapot. They hadn't, but the owner, who was out at that time, was contacted and within 30 minutes turned up with a newly purchased teapot and a hearty welcome. That's Australia for you!

Alice, as it is known colloquially, is situated in Australia's Northern Territory and roughly in Australia's geographic center, being equidistant from both Adelaide and Darwin. It has an arid environment, with the usually dry Todd River running through the center of town.

David discovered a postcard depicting an annual event called Henley on the Todd, which showed a photograph of a number of boats, including an old eight-man rowing shell with their bottoms knocked out and their rowers standing in the boats, holding the boats up around their waists by the gunwales while running the course of the race along the dry river bed.

He couldn't resist mailing one to the rowing club back in Daytona Beach.

Alice Springs was, in David's opinion, fabulous. It was small, hot and in fact very much like the small towns where he had lived and worked in Rhodesia.

There was a small tourist industry, several small shops including a well-stocked supermarket, a barber and plenty of pubs. There were many aborigines living there, although none of them seemed to work. They were mostly seen in parks and public areas, men grouped under one tree and women under another.

The town was within easy walking distance from their hotel and there was a very clean but barely used bus service which they used only once. It appeared to David that the aborigines seemed content to receive a government subsidy and to stay out of the way rather than become involved in the community, somewhat similar to the Inuit in Canada.

The famous Ayers Rock, now given to and controlled by the aborigines and renamed Uluru, was on David's agenda and was accessed by boarding a huge bus with giant fenders and traveling for six hours on a small road. A group of tourists, mostly Australians, came aboard, and refreshments in the form of bottled water were provided en-route.

The rock, actually a large sandstone formation sacred to the aboriginal people of the area, was so huge that it could be seen for about an hour before reaching it. Their journey was mainly through sparse undergrowth and fairly flat desert No wildlife, not even kangaroos or wallabies were sighted, which was a surprise, but several large flocks of colorful budgerigars were seen.

Upon arriving at Uluru, the group was allowed to walk all around it but, unlike in the old days, were not allowed to climb onto it. A chain handrail was still in place to assist climbers in reaching the top, but under aborigine control, this was strictly forbidden. There were some ancient paintings that could be seen on the rock and Uluru is listed as a UNESO World Heritage Site.

Once his group had circumnavigated the rock, they were taken to a patch of desert about two miles away, which David recognized as being the spot where Lady Diana, Princess of Wales, was photographed seated on a small piece of sandstone, gazing wistfully at distant Ayers Rock. David talked Bonnie into climbing the barbed wire fence and striking the same pose for a photograph that came out perfectly.

A 'barbie', consisting of sausages—referred to as steak on a stick—and a variety of salads were then provided by the tour organizers before they headed back to Alice Springs in the dark. On the return journey, their driver barely avoided running into a herd of camels crossing the road. This explained the giant fenders which adorned the fronts of all the buses.

Although they spent a week in Alice Springs, they never did encounter any springs! However, they did learn a lot about life in the Australian outback before boarding The Ghan and heading north to Darwin.

After another uncomfortable night in their seats, they disembarked at their final destination but had some difficulty in finding accommodation in Darwin and eventually settled for a small room in a youth hostel.

The town of Darwin is small, although considerably larger than Alice Springs. The plan was to spend two or three days there before catching a flight to Cairns and the Great Barrier Reef. However, a serious cyclone had struck Cairns while they were in Darwin and they were dissuaded from traveling there.

This left them with two choices—visit their Coffee Bay friends who had since emigrated from Johannesburg to Perth on Australia's west coast or travel to Bali in Indonesia. They chose the latter, having heard so many good reports from other travelers.

Bali was interesting but disappointing. Not only was it very crowded, but the beaches were dirty and littered with debris. The local authorities had dozens of workers out on the beaches early each morning cleaning up rubbish that had been washed ashore, allegedly from neighboring Java, but despite tourism making up 80 percent of its economy, this wasn't the Bali of legend.

Their hotel was in Denpasar and very close to the beach; their room was comfortable and the staff very obliging. Denpasar was a busy and very crowded town with shops offering a wide range of goods and services, many geared to the affluent and somewhat kinky tourist trade.

They hired a taxi for three of the seven days that they were there and their driver, who spoke reasonable English, did take them to some quiet, out-of-the-way places that were much more attractive.

They also saw many banyan, coconut, bamboo and acacia trees and many hibiscuses, frangipani, bougainvillea, poinsettia, oleander, jasmine, water lily, lotus and begonias. Bali had all the makings of a beautiful tropical paradise spoiled only by its excessive population and the littering that it creates.

It was their driver who introduced them to the crab-eating macaques or monkeys. They were known locally as *kera* and were quite common around settlements and temples where they had become accustomed to being fed by humans. They are quite often kept as pets by the locals.

Upon returning to Darwin, they decided to fly to Brisbane, hire a car and drive back to Sydney. Once a car had been rented, they drove south along the coast road and within an hour came across a small town called Surfer's Paradise in Queensland.

They began looking for some waterfront accommodation and luckily found a high-rise timeshare apartment with a magnificent view of the beaches and ocean. They were soon out exploring this colorful little town and were amazed at how clean, new and well maintained everything was. The sandy beaches were groomed and the lush green lawns that separated the beach from the main road were beautifully manicured.

There were meandering footpaths and a running/cycling track alongside the beach, several new clean and modern toilets and showers and every hundred yards or so there were gas fired, stainless steel barbecues, apparently for use at no charge to the general public.

The town itself, although small, had an abundance of restaurants, pubs and shops and seemed to be teeming with young, well-behaved people. This was truly paradise. Each morning while they were there, David would don his running gear and take a five-mile run along the oceanfront.

When they departed, he'd decided that of all the places in Australia, Surfers Paradise was the one that he liked the best.

The drive south to Sydney was interesting and picturesque and prior to returning to Florida, their visit wouldn't have been complete without spending a day at Bondi Beach. The beach was crowded, clean and had excellent facilities, which explained why it was so popular. A beautiful ending to a terrific holiday.

Later that same year, David began participating in five and ten kilometer races and half marathons organized by the Daytona Area Running Series. In 2011, then 67, he competed in the full series for the first time.

In 2015, having earned five trophies for being the fastest man in his age group for five consecutive years, he was inducted into the Daytona Running Series Hall of Fame, an honor in name only for there is no actual hall! In fact, for seven successive years, he was the fastest runner in his age group and won many trophies and awards.

A few years later, at the age of 68, he became tired of rowing. He was having difficulty keeping pace with the younger men and resigned from the club and bought a kayak. He was still on the water, still having fun and happy to be looking forward, which is what one does in a kayak, rather than backward, which one does in a rowing shell.

His Shepherd's Bush pal, Ken, who lived just down the street, was an avid kayaker and was delighted to have David join him three mornings a week for some wild and wacky paddling through the Florida mangroves and waterways.

David discovered that kayaking in central Florida provided a wonderful opportunity to appreciate the peace and tranquility of the tiny waterways that permeate this mangrove-laden area. Three mornings each week, they were watching dolphins at play and were fascinated by the huge and ungainly but very placid manatees leisurely enjoying life.

The area abounded with a myriad of birds from bald eagles to the great blue heron, the occasional pair of roseate spoonbills, and flocks of huge white pelicans migrating from their chilly northern habitats during the winter months.

Alligators were encountered from time to time, mainly on the upper reaches of Spruce Creek or on the St. John's River, as their preference is for fresh water rather than the brackish waters nearer the coast.

David thankfully found the alligator to be far timider than its cousin, the Nile Crocodile, and kayaking was a great relief from all the hustle and bustle of Masters rowing—but alas, no medals!

Before taking any more overseas trips, David decided to apply for United States citizenship. He was tired of having to stand in a different line from Bonnie when re-entering the country, and so in due course became a citizen of the United States with a new passport to prove it. This was number four! When would it ever end?

Chapter Eighteen

Around 2013, the U.S. economy was in the doldrums and sales at art shows had dropped off to the point that they were no longer viable. David continued his weekly attendance at the Art League, but after selling most of his artwork, he decided to discontinue painting and sold his framing equipment.

In 2014, after a brief stop in England, they visited Greece and took their first voyage on the Windstar Line. The *Windstar*, the flagship of the fleet, is a sailing and motor yacht over 400 feet in length with four masts and self-furling sails.

Their journey was to take them through the Aegean Sea to Turkey before disembarkation in Istanbul. Although the Windstar Line has several small cruise ships, the *Windstar* is, in David's opinion, the best one.

Before sailing, they spent a few days in Athens, taking time to view plaster casts of the original Elgin marbles. They had made a point of visiting the British Museum when in London prior to flying to Athens and saw the original marbles. Made in the fifth century BC, they were apparently excavated and allegedly pilfered by agents of Thomas Bruce, 7th Earl of Elgin in the early 19th century and transported by sea to Britain in order to decorate his house.

The marbles are actually a collection of sculptures made from marble from Mount Pentelikon, and at the time when viewed by David, they were a major point of contention between the British and Greek governments.

The rooftop restaurant of their hotel in Athens provided a magnificent view of the Parthenon on the Acropolis, where the marbles originated. The view was especially appealing at night when this famous and ancient structure was beautifully illuminated, so that was another must-see location.

The following day, upon visiting this ancient citadel, which is located on a large rocky outcrop above the city, David was surprised to learn that the Parthenon and other surrounding buildings sustained much of their damage not by erosion over the ages but during a 1687 siege by the Venetians during the

Morean War, when gunpowder being stored by the then Turkish rulers in the Parthenon was hit by a Venetian bombardment and exploded.

Athens is one of the world's oldest cities, with its recorded history spanning over 3,000 years. It is a large cosmopolitan metropolis with a population close to 4 million, yet David was amused to see how many stray dogs were seen in and around the Athens city center. Each dog seemed to have claimed its own street corner and the locals took it upon themselves to keep the animals well fed.

Having seen a good deal of Athens and its people, they boarded their yacht and set sail. Their journey through the Aegean Sea included stopping at several islands, notably Mykonos, Rhodes and Santorini. They enjoyed a multitude of Greek experiences, including taking a mule ride to reach the top of Santorini and will never forget its classic Cycladic architecture, whitewashed cubed houses with blue shutters and small Greek orthodox churches that dotted the landscape.

Santorini is a member of Greece's Cyclades islands, the most famous island chain in the Aegean Sea and also the site of one of the largest volcanic eruptions in recorded history, which occurred over 3,000 years ago. David found the island swarming with tourists from all parts of the world, which diminished the otherwise perfection of the island.

Santorini would be David's favorite of all the islands but, not to take anything away from those other islands, he insists that they were all positively delightful.

The *Windstar* yacht itself is very small by cruise ship standards, with a little over 100 passengers and almost as many crews. Entertainment was limited but excellent, with a small band featuring a fantastic balalaika player as its star performer. As they approached Turkey, a beautiful and talented belly dancer was brought on board to perform, a belly dancer whom David will never forget and whom he dreams of regularly.

From the Greek islands, their next port of call was in Turkey, where they spent a day touring the ancient and newly excavated Roman city of Ephesus. Although most of the city is still buried underground and well protected from the environment, the several acres that have been excavated are absolutely incredible.

Originally built by the Greeks in the 10th century BC, it apparently didn't really flourish until after it came under the control of the Roman Republic in

129 BC. Mosaic paved sidewalks, an ancient library, communal toilets with an innovative flush system and two amphitheaters were just some of the 3,000 year old wonders that have been uncovered and are in the process of being restored.

From Ephesus, they were taken to a carpet manufacturer, where the most exotic and intricate carpets were made. Although they insisted that they had no intention of buying a carpet, they were given a first-class presentation of carpet after carpet—huge carpets piled two feet high were flung aside one after the other, some made of silk, some double-sided and all handmade.

They were also shown how the silk threads were made. Silkworm cocoons were floated in a large vat of boiling water before beginning the process of meticulously peeling off one long filament of silk (one single thread was over 300 feet long) from the soggy cocoon and turning it into silk thread, which was then dyed and spun before being woven into carpets.

David felt rather bad at not making a purchase, especially as they had each been provided with a cup of tea, but the prices were in the tens of thousands of American dollars and in any case, they had no need for a carpet.

Their final destination and point of disembarkation was Istanbul, where they spent a few nights at the prestigious Para Palace Hotel.

Formerly known as Constantinople, Istanbul is the largest city in Turkey and straddles the Bosporus Strait, lying in both Europe and Asia. They found the city to be a thriving business center, and the residents were well dressed and appeared just as affluent as their counterparts in other European cities.

Istanbul features a large open square surrounded by shops and a huge temple, and tall minarets are used to project the frequent Muslim call to prayer. The square was teeming with individuals selling a variety of trinkets and tickets for various trips, including pleasure craft cruises along the Bosporus.

David and Bonnie were impressed by one ticket seller who spoke very good English and claimed that he was a Kurd, newly arrived in Istanbul and seeking a better life for his family than that available to them back home, where the Turks considered the Kurds to be second-class citizens. The vendor, whose name was Mustapha, claimed to be an English teacher but was reduced to hawking cruise tickets to tourists as his only means of sustenance.

They purchased two tickets from him and the following day enjoyed their boat tour along the Bosporus toward the Black Sea and back, passing beneath the huge bridge that connects Europe to Asia.

Their visit to Istanbul would not have been complete without going to the Grand Bazaar. This huge bazaar consists of street upon street of shops, restaurants, cafes and churches and is completely enclosed, covering over 400,000 square feet. The shops sell virtually everything: gold, carpets, lamps, silk and clothing, to name just a few.

Shopkeepers stand in their doorways, inviting potential buyers inside for tea and promoting their wares, stressing that their prices are the lowest and the quality of their goods the highest.

Their sales pitch must work, as Bonnie bought several silk scarves as gifts to take home and a beautifully made purse for herself. David was left to do the haggling, for he was warned beforehand that not to haggle is tantamount to an insult.

They also attended a spectacular show held in a small disused Roman ruin with several actors and dancers performing a series of dances, which included the whirling dervishes, all of which harkened back 2,000 years in time.

Prior to attending the show, they went for dinner at a nearby restaurant and took a table on the patio. When studying the menu, David ordered his usual lamb chops, but Bonnie came across something different called chicken chops. Always keen on trying something new, she ordered the chicken chops.

While they sat enjoying a glass of wine, David commented that, unlike Athens, where stray dogs abounded, there was an abundance of stray cats everywhere in Istanbul, including on the patio where they were seated.

"Look at all these cats. They all look happy, friendly and well fed, but they're all young cats. You never see any old cats!"

Needless to say, Bonnie didn't eat her chicken chops when they arrived.

***

Upon returning to Florida, David began making plans for their next holiday and settled on a second trip to South Africa. Consequently, in 2017 they flew to Cape Town via the United Kingdom but instead of touring the entire country they remained in Cape Province and rented an apartment for six weeks in Hout Bay.

Just an hour's drive south of Cape Town, Hout Bay is a small fishing village in a wonderful setting with the mountain of Chapman's Peak on the shoreline.

David and Bonnie settled into a routine where she would attend fitness classes each morning while he ran the very steep and rugged pathway to the top of Chapman's Peak and back.

On one of his morning runs, David met up with a fellow runner, a schoolteacher from Hamburg, Germany. He and his girlfriend became good friends with David and Bonnie for the rest of their stay, which made their holiday even more memorable.

Plans were made for their German friends to visit Florida, but the arrival of the Covid pandemic a few years later put paid to that and while they remain in touch, their friends have yet to cross the Atlantic.

This, interspersed with visits to the Stellenbosch wineries and to some good friends living in the coastal town of Hermanus, along with plenty of reading and some excellent nature programs on TV, kept them both busy. Having a regular routine gave them a taste of living in Cape Province, although they did take a few days to drive north up the Garden Route which they had found fascinating on their previous visit.

Along the way, they spent two nights at a private game reserve named Bottlierskop, where their very personable African guide Silas took them on some extraordinary tours viewing lion, rhino, giraffe, zebra and a variety of antelope. When hearing that they were headed to Addo, well known for its large elephant population, he made a point of telling them that the elephant was his favorite animal and to give them his best wishes.

Their accommodation at Bottlierskop was a comfortable thatched cottage which could only be reached by crossing a small river. There was no bridge but instead a pontoon which, once boarded, they could pull themselves across with a rope. There were lions in the area, so it was important to keep a sharp eye open and not to venture out after dark.

Washroom facilities took the form of an outdoor shower and bathtub, which also proved interesting! Bonnie could be a pest at times, especially when she had her camera handy and it would have served her right if a wandering lion had caught her in the act of photographing David in the altogether getting all soaped up!

From Bottlierskop, they journeyed further north to Addo Elephant National Park, which, although it contained a variety of game, was primarily an elephant habitat. They spent four days at Addo in a small but comfortable bungalow and on one memorable occasion drove out at dusk to a water hole some ten miles from their lodging. Parking their vehicle quite close to the water, they were the only vehicle present and there were no animals in sight.

After 15 minutes or so, David pointed over to the left where a herd of some 50 elephants came crashing out of the thick bush, perhaps 500 yards away. David was used to seeing herds of elephants, but this herd was different. There was a lot of trumpeting, rumbling and squealing going on, but the large matriarch in the lead was obviously intent on leading her herd to their watering hole.

David, in his know-it-all fashion, wrongly declared that this was typical behavior of elephants bringing one of the herds to die.

They watched enthralled as the herd came closer and then stopped right in front of their small car. The herd consisted of cows and calves only, no bulls, and sure enough, one of the cows lay down not 20 feet in front of their car. All the other elephants were in an uproar, squealing and grumbling when a baby elephant appeared out of the prostrate cow.

Other cows gathered around the newborn and its mother, nudging both of them with their trunks until first the mother and then the baby staggered to their feet. The baby elephant moved instinctively between its mother's front legs, reached up, and began suckling.

Within 30 minutes the entire herd moved back through the trees from which they had come, the newborn baby elephant quite competently rambling along beneath its mother as darkness fell. An unforgettable and remarkable experience. They sent the elephants Silas's best wishes.

David learned afterwards that elephants, by placing the tips of their trunks on the ground and making loud rumbling noises, actually transmit vibrations for several miles to other elephants—in this case, announcing the new arrival. A kind of elephant Morse code, if you will.

With another African safari successfully complete, they flew home to Florida where David resumed his routine of run, cycle, kayak...repeat!

***

Later that year, the Halifax rowing club sent a mixed eight crew to Boston to compete in the Head of the Charles. This is a huge regatta that attracts well over 1,000 crews from all over the United States and is staged over a three-mile course on the Charles River. Bonnie was coxswain of the HRA's mixed eight and David, as a spectator, decided to run the footpath alongside the racecourse.

While the rest of the crew decided to fly up to Boston, David and Bonnie chose to leave several days earlier and drive. Their journey took them northwest to Niagara Falls, which neither of them had seen before and having crossed into the Canadian side they were able to see the falls in their full majesty.

Once in Canada, they drove north to Quebec before crossing back into the United States. All the trees were in their full autumn colors and the drive through New England down to Boston was truly magnificent.

Race day was cold but bright and sunny. Halifax put in a respectable time but did not medal and David, although passed by the crew on his run up to the start, didn't see them on the way back.

On their drive back to Florida, they saw considerable storm damage to buildings and trees caused by a hurricane that had swept through while they were away. Timing is everything!

It was around this time that they decided to sell their Port Orange house on the river and downsize. This took over a year, but they eventually sold and bought a much smaller and more manageable property in nearby New Smyrna Beach.

Chapter Nineteen

New Smyrna Beach is a delightful town first settled by Europeans in 1768 and named New Smyrna by Dr. Andrew Turnbull in honor of his wife's birthplace, which was the Ottoman (now Turkish) city of Smyrna.

The quaint and historic town center straddles the Intracoastal Waterway with two bridges connecting the west side of the river to the beach. The area offers many opportunities for outdoor recreation, including water sports of all kinds and is ranked as one of the world's Top 20 surf towns by *National Geographic*.

It is also dubbed 'The Shark Bite Capital of the World', although, in comparison with the shark bites that David knows of in South Africa and has heard of in Australia, New Smyrna's shark bites are but mere nibbles.

When David and Bonnie moved there in 2017, the population was less than 30,000 and they were disappointed to see how many new housing developments the city had planned.

***

In 2017, another trip was planned, this time to China. Flying into Shanghai, they stayed in a hotel on the Bund, originally a banking district established by the British in the mid-1800s. The Bund is a waterfront area that faces modern skyscrapers on the opposite shore and contains many magnificent old commercial buildings.

Walking through the area in which their hotel was situated, David was interested in seeing how advanced and modern everything seemed to be, although some of the elegant old buildings on the Bund appeared rather run down. Virtually no one was without a cell phone, the people were well dressed and many young people were in evidence.

Roads were as good as any he had seen anywhere and motor vehicles were the same as one might see in the United States, perhaps rather smaller but most appeared to be recent models.

The road system in Shanghai seemed decent, but it was crowded everywhere. Drivers, cyclists and motorcyclists all vying for space and pedestrians all pushing, shoving and elbowing their way through the crowds. It appeared as though no one had any manners, but perhaps that's the Chinese way.

They met up with their guide for the Viking cruise and although well-spoken and quite humorous, David suspected he was an undercover operator for the Chinese intelligence service. He referred to him as the lollipop man for the duration of their stay—wherever they went, he held a long stick above his head that had a large, colored disc on top, reminiscent of a lollipop. David conceded that it was a well-conceived method of not losing his party in crowded places.

Their guide escorted them on their flight from Shanghai to Wuhan, a huge city of over 11 million, but they didn't get the opportunity to see anything of the city as they were ushered immediately onto their Viking ship for a week-long voyage north up the longest river in Asia, the Yangtze, to Chongqing.

Their Viking ship, named the *Emerald*, was much bigger than expected but appeared to be quite old and certainly a step down from their experience with the *Windstar*.

As they passed along the busy waterway, David saw huge skyscrapers being built, cities being developed and construction on an unparalleled level. The river was full of shipping and tugs drawing barges full of cement, girders and construction materials of all description. This was most definitely a country on the move.

It took a long time to pass through the enormous lock system of the Three Gorges Dam, which is the largest dam in the world. The gorges themselves consist of three adjacent gorges along the middle reaches of the Yangtze River and, in David's view, they are absolutely awe inspiring as they span 183 miles. The surrounding countryside, mountainous and very scenic, was certainly quite different from that seen by David in his previous travels.

Once through the locks, they encountered many large towns and cities and by the time they reached Chongqing, they had made several shipboard friends, which made it all the more enjoyable.

Chongqing, which one would have thought to be perhaps the largest city in the world with a population of over 16 million, is actually the fourth most populous city in China after Shanghai, Beijing and Shenzhen.

Their voyage completed, they flew to Lhasa in Tibet, which, at almost 12,000 feet, is one of the highest cities in the world. Many people, including Bonnie, experience altitude sickness. Their hotel in Lhasa had a full-time doctor on staff who administered oxygen and various fluids to counteract the altitude sickness, but unfortunately this treatment took almost 24 hours to fully take effect.

David was pleased to see clear air and blue skies in Tibet after the overcast skies that he had experienced so far and found the city of Lhasa dominated by the huge Potala Palace, somewhat distant and high above the city. This was the home of the 14th Dalai Lama until he fled after a 1959 uprising and sought refuge in India.

Their guide took them on a tour of the Potala Palace, on which construction started in 1645. With over 1,000 rooms, 10,000 shrines and about 200,000 statues, the palace is absolutely huge and awe inspiring. The sloping stone walls were almost 10 feet thick, with a base as thick as 16 feet. Quite a building.

The city of Lhasa was rural and relaxing. The buildings appeared to be mainly constructed of wood rather than concrete and the people, although healthy in appearance and cheerful in nature, appeared far less sophisticated than the Chinese they had encountered elsewhere.

The food consisted primarily of yak and vegetables, a yak being a very hairy sort of oxen. It didn't taste very good but the food in China was, according to David, who is no connoisseur of good food, pretty awful anyway.

Lhasa had a huge central square with several large outdoor furnaces spewing clouds of incense-like smoke. This smoke became so intense that everyone resorted to buying face masks. David suggested that perhaps the numerous face mask retailers were the ones keeping the furnaces going to give their sales a boost!

They had the opportunity to visit several Buddhist monasteries and David recalls that at one particular location it appeared that over a 100 presumably hopeful young monks, many of whom were really just boys, were seated on the ground attending some sort of lecture.

They all wore identical mauve or purple gowns and had shaved heads, but they appeared to be anything but devout. Most of them appeared to be paying absolutely no attention to their lecturer; they were whispering to each other, giggling and generally playing the fool. David was not impressed.

After an enjoyable few days in Lhasa, they flew to Xi'an, where the famous ancient terracotta warrior statues had been excavated. Inside several huge and very substantial buildings were literally hundreds of life-sized terracotta soldiers—each one different in facial expression.

Uniforms varied to some degree and some were mounted on terracotta horses or driving terracotta chariots. Although David had seen films and photographs of the Xi'an site, to be present and see the real thing was absolutely astounding.

This army was buried with Qin Shi Huang, the first emperor of China in 209 BC, to protect him in his afterlife. It is estimated that the three pits contain approximately 8,000 soldiers plus 130 chariots and over 250 horses, the majority of which still remain buried.

Again, parts of the display area were so overcrowded, with much pushing and shoving, that David just stayed outside until the rest of his tour joined him.

Incredibly, the terracotta figures were only discovered in 1974 by local farmers. David hopes that they were well rewarded.

While in Xi'an, they saw an opera that was very colorful and dramatic and which they enjoyed immensely.

From Xi'an, they flew to Beijing, where they were accommodated in the best hotel David had ever stayed in, the Fairview Hotel. The dining facilities were excellent, the room first class, but the bathroom was superb, especially the toilet.

It was a sort of toilet/bidet combination with a small keyboard at the side, which one used to control a jet of water across a broad selection of temperatures, at a variety of angles and at different pressures. This experience was one of the highlights of David's trip!

After this delightful taste of the Orient, David was very reluctant to leave his hotel room, but arrangements had been made to visit the Great Wall of China so they drove there with their guide and his small group. What an experience. The wall is so long and so enormous that it defies belief.

The entire wall spans sixteen provinces and although only some parts of it remain, the 'small' section closest to Beijing is almost 500 miles long. To reach the top of the wall was quite a climb, but once there the view was magnificent and David could see the wall as it snaked mile after mile through valleys and over hills until it disappeared into the distance.

David describes Beijing as a modern and vibrant city that, contrary to popular belief, had little if any air pollution, at least while they were there. The local parks were lush and green, with plenty of groups practicing Tai-chi.

In one park, they saw a number of beautiful giant pandas chewing contentedly on sticks of bamboo in their separate enclosures and in another area a playful group of the delightful if smaller red pandas were tumbling and chasing each other. A very peaceful scene.

In fairness to their Chinese tour guide, David feels that he should be given credit for going to great trouble to show them the other side of life in Beijing. They were taken on a tricycle rickshaw ride through a rough and seedy, almost slum-like area of the city and visited a family in their home. While clean and reasonably comfortable, it was a far cry from the modern facilities that they had been exposed to throughout most of their journey.

After visiting Tiananmen Square and the imposing Forbidden City, where huge portraits of Chairman Mao glowered down at them, their Viking tour was complete. They then had a week to explore by themselves and flew down to the small town of Guilin in southern China, a relatively small town renowned for its beautiful scenery.

Left to arrange their own accommodation, David chose a two-star hotel in downtown Guilin, which turned out to be a mistake. After two nights at the magnificent Fairview Hotel, their new hotel had a desk staff member who couldn't speak English and reluctantly, after much gesticulating and harsh words, gave them a grotty room upstairs with hookers frequently knocking on the door and sliding their business cards beneath it when no one answered.

The following day was much better. After checking out of the hotel from hell, they made their way to the busy and touristy downtown, and while seated at an outside table on the busy main street enjoying a beer, a young Chinese couple walked by with a little girl.

The little girl kept staring at Bonnie, who gave her a wave. The girl waved back and then came over to speak with her. Her English was perfect and when her parents came over to join them, it turned out that they lived in the United States and were just back in China on holiday.

After they left, three scruffy-looking men seated at a nearby table approached with cameras. They appeared to be out-of-towners, perhaps on a visit to the big city, and although they spoke no English, they made it clear that they wanted to take photographs seated next to Bonnie and each took turns sitting next to her and having their photo taken.

It turned out that it was her blonde hair that was the attraction; she was probably the only blonde in Guilin and possibly the first one they had ever seen.

David and Bonnie later hired a young woman to take them on a local tour on her three-wheeled motor scooter—she was at the front while they sat on a bench behind her. She wasn't a very good driver and spoke very little English, but the tour was pleasant and their guide was very personable.

Another experience was when they went out on the river at night to accompany the fishermen. Each fisherman had his own small wooden craft containing a few baskets and three or four cormorants. Once out on the river, the cormorants, with a tight metal collar around their necks, were released into the river to catch fish.

The cormorants could not swallow the fish because of the restrictive collar, so they returned to the boat where the fisherman retrieved the fish and sent the bird back into the water to catch another one. It should be noted that at the end of the evening, the birds' collars were removed and they were rewarded with a few fish.

Apparently, cormorants are so successful at catching fish that the authorities have had to impose limits on the hours when the fisherman can use them and the number of fish that can be harvested. An absolutely fascinating spectacle.

From Guilin, they took a beautiful four-hour boat ride on the Li River to the even smaller town of Yangshuo. Unfortunately, the journey was spoiled by rain for most of the journey, plus the boat was very crowded and full of noisy locals with lots of shouting even though they were only a couple of feet apart.

Much to David's chagrin, when boarding the boat his Swiss Army knife was found in one of their suitcases and confiscated—or in his words—stolen.

They had previously booked accommodation at the Hidden Dragon Hotel. The hotel had about 30 rooms but was almost empty, so they were given an excellent room at the front of the hotel overlooking some fish farms and the river with an astounding if somewhat hazy view of the far distant blue, purple and pink mountains.

Someone with a hang glider or possibly a small ultralight was playing in the thermals off in the distance.

They spent three days at the Hidden Dragon Hotel exploring the area. Yangshuo is a resort destination for both domestic and foreign travelers. The language barrier was no problem as it seemed that everyone in China had a cell phone which they spoke into in Chinese and an English translation emerged, and vice versa. Modern technology is incredible and way over David's head, who incidentally does not have a cell phone.

From Yangshuo, it was on to Hong Kong, where it rained non-stop for two days. The one saving grace was that David was able to purchase a new Swiss Army knife and Bonnie, who has tiny feet, was delighted to find so many shops with a wide variety of tiny shoes, so all's well that ends well. Although the weather didn't cooperate, they took a ferry across Victoria Harbor where they boarded the popular Red Bus tour of Kowloon.

What little they did see of Hong Kong showed them it was a huge, modern city with a thriving economy. There appeared to be plenty of tourist destinations, but due to the inclement weather their activities were mainly limited to shopping.

David's overall impression of China was obviously that of a rapidly growing superpower doing an excellent job of improving the lot of its huge but relatively poor population. From the perspective of a western tourist taking a holiday there, the crowds, the pushing and shoving and the food were a disappointment.

In some ways, he found it similar to visiting a third world country, while in others, its technology and infrastructure were comparable to the best that the West can offer.

Recovering from the China trip took David some time as he rationalized the good, the bad and the ugly, but after a few months he was ready to hit the road again. Life at home seemed rather dull and therefore a trip to Ireland was envisaged.

Ireland was a country that David had never been to before even though it was where his mother's family, the Ronaynes, had originated.

Following a few days with Sister Linda in Hampshire, flying into Dublin airport was a bit chaotic, as their aircraft was put in a holding pattern due to several flights arriving at the same time.

After flying in circles for about fifteen minutes, their pilot announced that they were running low on fuel and would be crossing the Irish Sea again, this time to Liverpool to refuel and off they went, back the way they had just come.

After refueling, they crossed the Irish Sea for the third time and eventually landed, picked up a rental car and went to look for a hotel.

As luck would have it, the famous and world-renowned Riverdance performance was being staged in Dublin while they were there and that, together with a first-class tour of the city, was a treat to behold.

Virtually, all the pubs, and there were plenty, had Irish entertainment with a plethora of local folk music and ballads.

Their week spent in Ireland was absolutely wonderful and the weather beyond their wildest expectations. It was so warm and sunny that the locals were frequently heard complaining of a heatwave, while David and Bonnie thought it delightful.

They spent some time in Youghal, County Cork, where David's branch of the Ronayne family originated and where he sampled his first pint of truly Irish Guinness, a dark and creamy brew best sampled at just below room temperature, not refrigerated.

From Youghal, they traveled south to Killarney and circled the ring of Kerry, spending the night in Portmagee, a tiny and picturesque fishing village with brightly painted houses at the southwest tip of Valentia Harbor and close to the rugged and mountainous shoreline of southern Ireland with its magnificent cliffs, incredible scenery and hospitable people.

Not far offshore is small Puffin Island, off limits to visitors but home to thousands of puffins, hence the obvious name.

They then journeyed north up the west coast, spending a couple of nights at the magnificent cliffs of Moher. The cliffs run for about nine miles and range in height from just under 400 to over 700 feet and from the cliffs the Aran Islands can be seen in Galway Bay.

The cliffs rank among the most visited tourist sites in Ireland, with well over a million visitors each year.

They then crossed to Waterford, a city first established by Viking invaders in 853 AD. The Vikings were driven out by the native Irish but returned in 914 AD and built what would be Ireland's first city.

David and Bonnie's main objective was to purchase some glassware from the famous Waterford lead glass or 'crystal' glassworks. Unfortunately, they found that the original manufacturing base on the edge of Waterford had closed down due to the insolvency of Waterford Wedgewood PLC, but they learned that a new location had recently reopened back in the city center.

They toured the new glassworks, watched men blowing beautiful crystal creations and purchased some whisky and hock glasses to take home.

While at the Waterford showrooms, David met Gerald, a gentleman who said he had a friend who was an ex-member of the BSAP. David only knew one Irishman in the Force and that was his squad mate 'Paddy' Finn.

Upon mentioning his name, Gerald's eyes lit up and he exclaimed, "It's him. I drink with him at our local pub just about every night."

He then phoned his friend and told him who he had bumped in to and they arranged to meet that evening at their local pub.

The pub in question was about 20 miles from Waterford, but Gerald gave David directions and said he would meet them there later.

David and Bonnie set off for Mother Molly's pub, but thanks to the Irishman's hopelessly confusing directions, they got lost in the maze of small, twisted roads, a nightmare to someone used to driving on North American roads for over 30 years.

After seeking help from several locals, they eventually located the small village which appeared to consist of nothing more than two pubs and a church. Upon entering the bar, which was almost empty, and asking the barman if he had seen Mr. Finn, he indicated a door leading into another bar and was told he'd find him in there.

It had been over 50 years since David had last seen Paddy, so he didn't know quite what to expect. Upon entering, the only person there was a well-dressed gentleman in jacket and tie who in no way resembled the Paddy Finn of David's youth. He addressed David in a broad Irish accent, saying that there had been a misunderstanding for his name was not Finn but Flynn.

However, he had served in the BSAP for sixteen years, had been stationed in Salisbury for all of that time and was certainly there at the same time as David. They spoke of many mutual acquaintances and relived many Rhodesian experiences of old. The pleasant evening unfortunately ended rather early, as David and Bonnie had a long way to travel to get back to their hotel in County Cork.

With very happy memories of Ireland, the country, the warm and friendly people and their experience well beyond their expectations, they flew via London to Barcelona.

They hired a car and, over a period of one month, drove down the coast road through many magnificent resort towns on the Costa Brava and Costa del Sol to Gibraltar and Portugal.

They found Barcelona to be a most magnificent city and of special interest was the large pedestrian mall, which virtually divides the old town into two and is named La Rambla. The avenue stretches from the port and is lined with numerous restaurants, shops and outdoor cafes.

David was particularly impressed with the beer, which was served in one liter beer mugs.

Another feature of the city that was a revelation was Sagrada Familia, the largest unfinished Catholic church in the world. Designed by the long-dead Antoni Gaudi, it is part of a UNESCO World Heritage Site and was consecrated and proclaimed a minor basilica in 2010 by Pope Benedict XVI.

A huge line-up of visitors was present when David and Bonnie went there, but they persevered, waited patiently in line and eventually gained admission along with thousands of others.

Incredibly, construction began in 1882 yet, due to a series of wars, fires and vandalism, it was only just over half finished when they visited.

David was in full agreement with art critic Rainer Zerbst, who said, "It is probably impossible to find a church building anything like it in the entire history of art."

It's incredible spires and spiky design is like no other and it was still awaiting the addition of another ten spires. David doubted that the hopeful completion date of 2026 would be accomplished.

Moving south along the magnificent coast highway, they headed for the tourist mecca of Torremolinos, making one or two stops along the way. The town had been a poor fishing village before the growth of tourism which began in the late 1950s, but since then it has expanded enormously to over 60,000 inhabitants.

The beach extends for almost five miles, has cycle and skating lanes alongside the fully illuminated promenade and features many beach bars and restaurants. David had never seen so many bare breasts and bottoms in his life and that's saying something as one of his pastimes is painting nude models!

David recalls chatting with an English waitress in one of the restaurants who told them that she had come to Torremolinos six years previously for a holiday and never went home. She still didn't speak much Spanish but said it wasn't necessary because everyone speaks English.

From Torremolinos, they drove down to La Linea, for David couldn't resist a visit to Gibraltar and was amazed to learn that the easiest and most popular way of getting there was to leave the car and walk across from Spain, but this was no simple walk. The only airport runway on Gibraltar had to be crossed between aircraft taking off and landing!

Once on 'the rock', they enjoyed a leisurely lunch in the large town square and of course the visit just wouldn't have been complete without climbing to the top of the rock and saying hello to a few of its famous Barbary apes.

Before leaving Spain, they booked into a simply awful hotel in the small town of Tarifa and took a ferry across the Straits of Gibraltar to Tangier in Morocco, the westernmost country in the Maghreb region of North Africa.

Their hotel in Tangier, although very large and very old, had a wonderful view from its large verandah, but unfortunately, being Muslim owned it served no alcohol.

They had been given the name and email address of a Moroccan guide by some people they met in New Smyrna Beach and engaged him to show them around while visiting. He turned out to be excellent and made their stay unforgettable.

He showed them the sights and arranged for their driver to take them to the city of Chaoen, just inland from Tangier. This city, nicknamed the 'Blue City', was incredible for every building was painted in varying shades of blue.

The effect was absolutely wonderful but quite labor intensive, as the paint they used was similar to whitewash and frequently needed a new coat. It appeared as though all this painting was done by the women, which David thought was a wonderful idea—Bonnie, not so much!

The beaches that they visited were beautifully maintained and full of tourists. David and Bonnie rode camels on the beach and on the road, much to the consternation of several motorists. They had no idea how to steer their camels, but they seemed to know where they were going and returned them safely to their vehicle.

In gratitude for his excellent service, they took their guide out for dinner the evening before they left and when telling him that their next destination was the Algarve in Portugal, he suggested that they find time to visit the town of Cascais further up the coast and within easy reach of Lisbon.

Once back in Spain, they drove to the Algarve in southern Portugal and later, on the advice of their Moroccan guide, they journeyed further north to the small seaside town of Cascais, where they were able to secure a room in a waterfront hotel overlooking the ocean.

David was familiar with a form of singing unique to Portugal called fado. He had never heard it sung but believed it to be exceptionally passionate and heart rending, so he asked the concierge if there were any fado performances in town.

The helpful concierge made some enquiries and discovered that one small restaurant was featuring fado that very evening. A table was booked and directions to the restaurant were obtained. What followed was an experience that David would never forget.

David had some difficulty finding the restaurant, which was located in a dingy alleyway in a less than salubrious part of town and definitely not on the tourist route. The door was closed and the windows curtained, giving the impression that the premises were closed.

Upon opening the door, he discovered a dimly lit restaurant with about 30 tables, each with a tablecloth and candle. Every table was occupied except for the one they had reserved. They were greeted warmly, ordered a drink and accustomed themselves to the gloom.

Against the wall, not twelve feet from their table, rested two acoustic guitars: a regular Spanish guitar and a twelve-string Portuguese guitar. No stage, no spotlights and no performers. Were they in the right place?

While enjoying their wine and the general ambiance of the restaurant, two men took their seats and began playing the guitars—soft, intricate melodies that were very pleasing and certainly Iberian in nature. Then a tall, slim stranger appeared, a man casually dressed and very relaxed, probably in his early forties, who leaned against the back wall between the two musicians.

The guitar music softened and the stranger began to sing. David had never heard anything like it; the passion with which the singer performed was incredible, and the hair on David's neck and arms began to rise and he began to understand. This was fado.

After performing two or three songs, the singer took a break and they were served their meals, which turned out to be excellent. They also struck up an acquaintance with two ladies at the next table who, it turned out, were on holiday from Stockholm.

Once the meals were finished, there was more entertainment; this time the singer was an attractive young woman who gave an equally galvanizing performance. When the entertainment was over, David and Bonnie continued their conversation with the two ladies.

More wine was ordered and by the end of the evening, it was agreed that if either was in the other's neck of the woods, they would meet up again. What a wonderful evening!

On the overland drive back to Barcelona, David and Bonnie spent one day and two nights in the sword-making capital of the world, Toledo, which lies on the banks of the Tagus River. They discovered a wonderful old hotel right in the center of town and explored this amazing and historic city. He didn't come home with a sword but with a very impressive paper knife!

The manufacture of swords in the city of Toledo dates back to Roman times, but between the 15th and 17th centuries, the sword-making industry became such that the swords of Toledo were regarded as the best in Europe.

From Toledo, it was a long haul back to Barcelona, London and home. After such a lengthy holiday, they were happy just to relax, enjoy their home comforts and return to their domestic life of running, cycling, kayaking and playing cards on a Saturday night.

Chapter Twenty

Unfortunately, in 2018, at the age of 74, the onset of arthritis in his right hip put paid to David's running aspirations. To replace running, he purchased a bicycle and joined the ladies on their thrice-weekly bike ride, averaging up to 50 miles per week.

In the late spring of 2019, he took a break from his cycling and kayaking routine and he and Bonnie traveled to the Dutch city of Amsterdam, where they spent a few days, before boarding another Windstar vessel, only this time on a slightly bigger motor-powered yacht carrying about 200 passengers.

Amsterdam is full of bicycles and cyclists. Bikes are everywhere and the city's infrastructure is designed to accommodate them on all the major roadways—sometimes to the detriment of pedestrians, so watch where you walk! Amsterdam also has a wealth of canals, hence its reputation as another 'Venice of the North' (Saint Petersburg also claims this distinction).

The name Amsterdam originated when the Amstel River was dammed to control flooding and acquired the name Amstel Dam.

David's visit to Amsterdam would not have been complete without a visit to one of his favorite artist's house, studio and museum. He was amazed at the craftsmanship of Rembrandt's enormous rendition of *The Night Watch*, which he painted in 1642.

The huge tulip fields were reaching the end of their flowering season but were nonetheless spectacular and their visit to Keukenhof gardens was wonderful. Each autumn, 40 gardeners' plant 7 million bulbs in the park and the flowerbeds are synchronized to the different bulb flowerings to ensure there are blooms throughout the duration of the park's eight-week opening.

While in Amsterdam, they also walked Amsterdam's infamous Red Light district, but much to David's dismay, it was daytime and they were too early for any window displays.

Their yacht departed from Amsterdam and traveled to the small Dutch town of Harlingen, which lies on the coast of the Wadden Sea. They rented a couple of bicycles for a self-guided tour of the town and enjoyed a coffee, or in David's case tea, at a charming sidewalk café. David never has and never will drink a cup of coffee. To him, while the smell is bearable, the taste is awful.

From Harlingen, they paid a brief visit to Germany traveling along the huge Kiel Canal, which claims to be the busiest artificial canal in the world. How this can be justified is beyond reason when compared to the Suez or Panama canals, but that's what the brochures claim.

Their next port of call was Copenhagen, Denmark, but unfortunately the visit was a very short one and it rained the whole time they were there. Nevertheless, they did manage to see and photograph Copenhagen's famous mermaid.

From Copenhagen, their yacht paid a brief visit to Tallinn, Estonia, which is on the shore of the Gulf of Finland on the Baltic Sea. Estonia was occupied by the USSR after the German retreat in 1944 until it regained its independence and democracy returned in 1991. It is now the birthplace of many international high-tech companies and Tallinn was listed among the top ten digital cities in the world.

They then traveled further north to Saint Petersburg in Russia, where they spent two nights, had a wonderful guide and saw some spectacular sights. Rather than the dull and dreary city formerly known as Leningrad that they had expected, they found Saint Petersburg to be a clean, well laid out city, with several beautifully restored buildings.

The population of over 6 million was well dressed and friendly. The locals were courteous and not at all fond of Moscow or its politicians. The vehicles were on a par with those in the United States and in fact, there was more than a smattering of Mercedes Benz, Porsche and BMW.

In the 17th century, Saint Petersburg was named after Peter the Great, the Tsar who originally established the city. After the outbreak of World War I, it was renamed Petrograd and in 1924, following the death of Lenin, it was renamed Leningrad before returning to its original name, Saint Petersburg, in 1991.

The city is built on swamp and water and, for this reason, is often referred to as the 'Venice of the North' or the 'Russian Venice'.

David and Bonnie visited the Catherine Palace, which lies about 20 miles south of Saint Petersburg and is built on a hill. Work began on the existing palace in 1744, but major reconstruction took place in 1751. The palace, with its snow white columns and sky blue walls with gilded stucco, cupolas and sculptures, contains an alleged 200 pounds of gold!

Several additions and alterations have been made, but no matter how grand the palace once was, it was reduced to a shell when the German forces retreated after the Siege of Leningrad in World War II. They intentionally destroyed the interior of the palace, leaving just a shell.

Thankfully, the Russians have brilliantly restored the Catherine Palace to its former glory and the palace and its gardens are, in David's words, a sight to behold.

David and Bonnie then journeyed back to the city in one of several fast and modern hydrofoils that ply the waterway.

The Hermitage Museum was next on their list and they were amazed at its size. The largest art and culture museum in the world, the Hermitage was founded by Catherine the Great in 1764.

The museum has six historic and interconnected buildings along the Palace Embankment, including Catherine the Great's Winter Palace, which has a collection of antiques numbering in the millions, although only a small part is on display.

David claims that in the several hours they spent at the Hermitage, they saw so many examples of French, German, Swiss, British, Russian, Italian and Spanish fine art that he could not even begin to describe even a fraction of them. Not only were the collections overwhelming, but the beautifully restored buildings were a work of art in themselves with gold leaf covering virtually every doorway, archway and column.

Winding up their stay in Saint Petersburg, they attended an evening performance in the beautifully restored Mariinsky Theater, which was originally opened in 1860.

Seated in plush velvet seats at the very front of the second tier of seating, they had a magnificent view of the timeless *Swan Lake* performed by the Mariinsky Ballet. Having never attended a ballet before, David and Bonnie were absolutely enthralled, along with the packed audience.

David's experience in Russia and, for that matter China, was in total contrast to his expectations and not nearly as oppressive or regimented as he had been led to believe.

From Saint Petersburg, it was on to Helsinki in Finland just 50 miles north of Tallinn, which they had visited on their way north up the Baltic toward Saint Petersburg. Finland is considered to have one of the world's highest standards of living. Both Finnish and Swedish are the official languages, although David says that you may as well add English also for everyone there speaks it.

While walking the streets in Helsinki, David saw several signs pointing the way to a Lutheran church called the Church of the Rock or Rock Church.

Following these signs, they came to the church, the likes of which he had never seen before, for it was excavated into solid rock with a skylight surrounding a central copper dome, bathing the interior in natural light. The rough rock walls give the church excellent acoustics and because of this, it is frequently used as a concert hall.

They also spent a day on the small Finnish island of Mariehamn in the Åland Islands where Bonnie bought some delightful handmade earrings. David remembers the Finns complaining that the residents of Mariehamn thought of themselves as Swedish and actually spoke Swedish rather than Finnish.

From Mariehamn, they sailed south to Stockholm, where they spent a few nights in a central city hotel. The two ladies whom they had met in Portugal the previous year actually recommended the hotel to them, as it was centrally situated and not particularly expensive. The ladies met David and Bonnie at the hotel after breakfast and took them on a wonderful tour of the city and its environs.

Later that evening, they treated them to a meal in the old town, a historically important core of Stockholm in which motor vehicles are prohibited and which was originally built by the Vikings. David was allowed to provide a couple of bottles of wine, which he selected from a wine list written entirely in Swedish.

He must have selected the most expensive wine, for he finished up paying $100 US per bottle—more, he's sure, than the cost of the meal!

The following day, they strolled the city and visited the ABBA Museum, where they were able to re-live the excitement of the ABBA group in its heyday. It was interesting to note that even when paying for even the smallest item, Sweden was basically a cashless society. Everyone seemed to pay for everything with plastic.

The city of Stockholm stretches across 14 islands, where Lake Mälaren flows into the Baltic Sea. It is very clean and friendly and where the English language is spoken better than in England…a lot better.

From Stockholm, they flew home, crossed another few countries off their bucket list and talked about where to go next.

****

The last day of 2019 was David and Bonnie's 25th wedding anniversary and to celebrate, they went on another Windstar cruise in the Caribbean with some friends, visiting several of the islands and finding them warm, picturesque and welcoming but all so very similar. However, their cruise covered the entire New Year's holiday and was a wonderful way to wind up their first quarter of a century together!

Beginning and ending in St. Maarten, they visited St. Barthélemy, St. Kitts, and St. Lucia and, although enjoyable, didn't compare with their two earlier voyages with Windstar.

****

In early 2020, having just returned to Florida, David's kayaking pal and fellow Londoner Ken, decided that he and his wife Judy would emigrate from Port Orange to San Jose del Cabo, a small town very close to Cabo San Lucas at the southern tip of the Baja peninsula in Mexico and off they went, leaving David with no kayaking partner.

This was soon taken care of, however, as a neighbor of David's bought Ken's kayak and agreed to kayak with David every Saturday. The kayaks were secured on a friend's dock on the Halifax River and everything went well until their kayaks were stolen!

The culprits were eventually arrested and two of the three kayaks were recovered, but by this time two new kayaks had been purchased and were strapped and padlocked to the roof of David's Town and Country minivan, which stayed in his garage when not in use.

The minivan, with kayaks attached wherever he went, was soon to become a familiar sight in the neighborhood and came to be known in local circles as the kayakmobile.

Shortly afterwards Kevin, the young man who worked in David's sporting goods store back in 1963 until he was enticed to leave and see the world and was now 56, bought a 42-foot sailboat and set off from Central America to circumnavigate the world. The now middle-aged man and his boat, *Northern Pearl*, succeeded, taking a year to do it.

And in a satellite transmission from his cell phone as he was crossing the equator, he credited David with instilling in him a spirit of adventure some 37 years earlier, which made it all possible. Perhaps, thought David, he would get blamed if his voyage went awry!

Then Covid struck and all travel plans were put on hold for eighteen months. With kayaking once a week and cycling three times a week, David still had two mornings free and decided that walking would be an admirable way of filling the gap.

As background, on a recent visit to British Columbia, David's son Sean, who lived in a pretty lakeside cottage some 20 miles from the town of Chilliwack, had introduced him to a popular walking trail known to the locals as Teapot Hill. The trail to the top of the hill was rugged and quite steep and about two miles in length from top to bottom.

As they trudged up the hill, David noticed many teapots, some ceramic, some metal or enamel, hanging in the trees. It turned out that it was customary for people taking the trail to hang teapots along the way until the hill eventually became something of a tourist attraction and acquired its unusual name.

When returning home and having discovered a deeply wooded trail not far from his house, David began walking the trail with a friend Nancy who lived nearby, a woman who David had taught to row some ten or twelve years earlier and was very active and athletic. Nancy was an ex-CIA employee who, along with her husband, had traveled the world. She had an interesting past and was a good conversationalist.

Deviating somewhat from the subject, David often tells of the time when, coaching on the Intracoastal Waterway, this same lady happened to be a passenger in his small aluminum coach boat when they hit some rough water.

As they bumped along, she was propelled into the air and when she came down, she inadvertently stepped on the top of the boat's fire extinguisher, squirting foam directly into David's face. Everyone except him had a good laugh at his predicament and his comments to the lady in question are best left unsaid.

All was eventually forgiven and, getting back to the deeply wooded trail, David, recalling his earlier visit to Chilliwack's Teapot Hill, decided to name the trail Coffee Mug Trail and he and his friend began hanging coffee mugs on trees and bushes lining the route. This soon caught on and before long, well over 100 coffee mugs were to be seen, some in the most inaccessible locations.

David even made two elaborate signs that he planted at either end of the trail, but shortly thereafter they were removed, presumably by some narrow-minded or short-sighted half-wit who had no idea of the sense of quirky sentiment that they were destroying.

Constant and boring political debates and discussions regarding the upcoming presidential election marked 2020. By the end of the year, the incumbent was defeated and a new president was to take office early the following year. This did not go over very well with the outgoing president and frequent outbursts alleging election rigging and corruption were bandied about.

On 6 January 2021, just prior to the inauguration of America's new president, a mob of the outgoing president's supporters who numbered over 2,000, attacked and forced their way into the United States Capitol Building in Washington. They were apparently hoping to keep their president in power and during the course of the riot, five people died and many were injured, including 138 police officers.

David was shocked and saddened by this ridiculous and childish display and once again began to feel the stirrings of discontent with his present surroundings. A familiar case of itchy feet and an urge to move on came upon him, but it was tempered by the restraining hand of his soulmate, Bonnie.

***

At the beginning of 2022, with the Covid pandemic under control, David and Bonnie took their fourth Windstar trip, this time to French Polynesia in the South Pacific—and what a delightful surprise this turned out to be.

Firstly, everything David had ever heard about the wonderful, hospitable islanders of Tahiti and French Polynesia was true. No begging, no doorway shopkeepers hassling naive tourists to buy their wares; in fact, every aspect of their stay in Papeete was a delight. Having spent four days in Papeete and adjusted to the Polynesian way of life, they boarded their small Windstar yacht and visited several islands, including Bora Bora and Moorea.

They swam in the fantastically clear waters where schools of friendly stingrays and blacktip sharks abounded and listened to their various guides playing ukuleles, nose flutes and singing their delightful native songs.

In fact, one Tahitian guide so impressed David, playing melodic, calming and smooth Tahitian music with his nose flute, that he decided to buy one and give it a try.

The guide explained that the flutes were not for sale anywhere but were made by the individual players themselves. When the tour ended, the guide gave David his flute, accepting no payment. Beautiful people!

French Polynesia actually comprises 121 islands and atolls stretching over 1,200 miles of the Pacific Ocean. The group of islands containing Tahiti is also known as the Society Islands.

Having visited the Hawaiian Islands twice, David had to admit that James Michener had it right in his book *Hawaii*, when he suggested that missionaries and the United States in general had Americanized Hawaii to the detriment of the islanders.

The French, by comparison, seem to have left the islanders in the South Pacific much to their own beliefs and customs. It was no wonder that those mutineers on *The Bounty* decided to stay and headed for the small Pacific Island of Reunion rather than go home. They had it made!

***

There is one last trip before this travelogue is over, and that was a week that David and Bonnie spent visiting their old friends Ken and Judy who were now living in San Jose del Cabo on the Baja. The weather was warm, in fact somewhat similar to Florida, and their friends' house was modern, spacious and beautiful.

The neighbors for the most part were snowbirds from either Canada or the northern states and they all seemed to be reasonably wealthy.

Their friends were terrific hosts and took them to all the local points of interest and also on a delightful boat ride on the Sea of Cortez, where they saw many whales and calves cavorting and sounding.

David was disappointed to find the landscape so dry and barren, the only vegetation being giant cacti and bits of tumbleweed. There was, however, one luscious green blaze spread across the brown and sandy landscape. It was, of course, an eighteen-hole golf course.

***

In the latter part of 2022, one of the worst hurricanes to arrive in the United States struck central Florida with a vengeance. Thousands of people were left homeless and well over 100 were killed. Ian, as the hurricane was named, had an impact on David and Bonnie's lives, but nothing compared to others in the area and for that they were thankful. Flooding was the main issue in New Smyrna Beach and David lost his cherished kayakmobile to flood waters.

***

Another sad moment was the death of Queen Elizabeth II, David's queen. At the age of 96, she had died at the same age as his mother. She was the only British monarch he had known and had reigned since he was seven or eight years of age. He, and probably millions of other people, had judged their behavior by her standards, even though he and most others never emulated them.

***

Travel has been a major factor in David's life and at the time of writing, he'd visited over 40 countries on five continents, lived in five and had become a citizen of four of them, South Africa being the exception.

Every country he's lived in evokes different memories. England, of course, is deeply ingrained—firstly, because of his family; secondly, because of his education; thirdly, his growth into manhood; and fourthly, its lousy weather. Rhodesia was David's eye-opener on the world and, to some degree, his metamorphous.

The many weird and wonderful experiences while serving in the British South Africa Police, his marriage and the birth of his two sons, and the launching of his own successful business venture combined to change him from a callow youth into a mature adult.

South Africa was much kinder to him than expected; businesswise, it was certainly a huge success and familywise it was where his wonderful daughter was born.

David is proud of his three children. They are all capable of thinking for themselves and have turned out to be self-confident and strongly independent individuals.

Canada, although a total disaster for the first few years, eventually became the safe haven he sought when first deciding to leave the African continent in the mid-seventies and has provided a happy home for his ex-wife Joyce, their three children and five grandchildren. The United States has given him a terrific wife, wonderful weather and a great lifestyle.

His numerous holidays have all been memorable, but the things that stand out and will forever be ingrained in his memory will be his Christmas dinner of fresh crayfish in Coffee Bay with very good friends, seeing the birth of an elephant in front of him in Africa, watching a performance of *Swan Lake* in an old and beautifully restored theater in Russia, walking the ancient Roman city of Ephesus in Turkey and touring the North Island of New Zealand on his motorcycle.

David would tell you that from his experiences a much larger book could have been written, of the places he's visited, people he's met, friendships he's made and memories he cherishes. But not wishing to bore the reader with any more stories, suffice it to say that he has found that people the world over, with the possible exception of politicians and lawyers, are the salt of the earth.

The Russians, Chinese, Africans, Pacific islanders, Europeans, Australians and New Zealanders he has met have all been pleasant and welcoming, so why so much animosity and conflict exists is a mystery.

***

A couple of recent bright spots are worthy of mention. The first is when David, after undergoing two nasty operations for a torn rotator cuff in his right shoulder, went for his usual circular four-mile walk over the bridges in New Smyrna Beach.

With his arm in a sling and shortly after setting out, his shoelace came undone and was flapping around his ankles, threatening to trip him. Unable to tie his shoelace with only one hand, he hadn't gone very far when a young woman approached him, saying, "I'm a nurse and can't bear to see you in such difficulty." She knelt down, retied his shoelace and bid him a good day.

About two weeks later, he was again on his walk. Trying to cross the busy South Causeway at the traffic light, he pressed the pedestrian crossing button and waited for the 'walk' sign to light up. When the traffic stopped and the 'walk' sign was illuminated, he stepped off the curb only to be almost bowled over by a vehicle turning right onto the causeway from a side street. He lurched back onto the sidewalk and then tried again, but the same thing happened with another car.

On his third attempt, with the 'walk' sign now beginning its 30-second countdown, a third car, a small Jeep, tried to run him down. This time, he brazenly walked across the road in front of it, thinking of all the ambulance-chasing lawyers on TV bragging about how getting run down by a car was like winning the lottery.

Just as you would expect from any self-respecting Florida driver, he began honking for all he was worth, continually, while David, still encumbered with a sling on his right arm, gave him a left-handed finger and directed a few choice words of Anglo-Saxon in return before safely reaching the other side of the road.

Three days later, when again on his walk, but this time with his walking partner, they saw a Jeep pull in ahead of them. A man stepped out and walked toward them.

The fellow approached and asked, "Are you the gentleman who was trying to cross at the lights last Friday?"

When David replied that yes, that was indeed him, the chap said, "I've been looking for you ever since and must apologize for my terrible behavior."

He then went on to say that David had the perfect right to punch him in the face right then and there.

Although tempted but somewhat incapacitated, David told the man, "Only one person in a million would do what you have just done," and forgave him sincerely.

David strongly believes that there are plenty of nice people in the world, even Americans, who, although collectively considered loud and brash throughout the world, are just as nice as anyone else when seen on their home turf.

It just seems incredible to him that so many countries fall into the grip of men who will never be convinced that they are wrong. They seem to believe their own lies because in their twisted minds, their lies are true. It doesn't matter what is true or false to others; their truth is all that counts and they will mislead, embellish and lie at every turn.

David was recently reminded of the British fascist Oswald Mosley, who he had learned about at school. Mosley apparently led a gang of 'Black shirts' prior to World War II who, as David understands, were no more than regimented bullies and thugs who wore their black shirts as a uniform.

Mosley was an outspoken supporter of Adolph Hitler before the war and was interned in the grounds of Holloway Prison from 1940 until 1943 and thereafter placed under house arrest and police supervision until the end of the war.

In 1959, Mosley, again trying to force his brand of politics on the British public, was soundly defeated in a British election, gaining less than 3,000 votes and thus losing the deposit that British politicians have to pay when standing for election. Mosley demanded a recount, claiming that the election had been rigged, and faded into obscurity.

David has seen similar performances in several African countries, in Russia, in South America and yes, even in the United States. Some people follow, just like sheep, or worse still, like lemmings. If the silent majority can't make themselves heard, he's afraid that our wonderful planet will self-destruct.

Putting lunatics aside, he believes that all the discontented souls out there who are wondering, as in that fabulous song by Peggy Lee, *Is That All There Is?* should perhaps throw caution to the wind but be careful where they tread. Remember, if you don't try, you'll never know—so be brave, take that next step and deal with the consequences.

It's worked for David so far and he can't help but wonder…

What's next?